RAISEYOUTHRIGHT

The Essential Career Planning Handbook for Teens

RaiseYouthRight

Contents

Preface

Decisions, decisions, decisions! That pretty much sums up being a teenager, right? You're learning to make choices that impact your life, from picking classes and electives to deciding who to chill with after school. And then there's the biggie: What do you want to be when you grow up? Suddenly, it feels like every decision is laying out the path for your future. It's thrilling, and yeah, let's not kid ourselves, it can be a bit scary too.

When I was a teen, the future seemed like a giant question mark. Which career should I chase? What if I pick the wrong one? And then there's the classic: what if my grades aren't shiny enough to get me into the college of my dreams? My mind was like a broken record, playing these worries over and over, sometimes even keeping me awake at night. Yeah, I was a fan of school and learning, but man, the pressure of figuring out my future was like carrying a giant backpack filled with textbooks.

In hindsight, I wish I knew then what I know now: that it's okay not to have everything figured out, that there are many paths to success, and that the "right" career is often discovered through a process of trial, and error. But as a teenager, it's hard to see beyond the pressure of the present moment.

That's why I've written this book. I want to help you navigate this exciting and sometimes daunting journey of career planning. Whether you have a clear vision for your future or no idea where to start, this book will provide you with the tools and guidance you need to make informed decisions about your career path.

Who Am I?

Hey there, I'm Richard Meadows. Once upon a time, I was in your shoes, trying to figure out where I fit in the grand scheme of things. The thoughts of "what's next after high school?" had me losing sleep. The weight of my folks' expectations, my teachers', and, let's be real, my own, felt like a backpack full of bricks. I wanted - no, needed - to make the right call and find a career that would lead me down the path to success and happiness.

Looking back, it's clear to me that my path wasn't just shaped by my choices. It was also formed by the experiences I stumbled into, the people I crossed paths with, and the exciting chances I grabbed when they popped up. The main takeaway? Career planning isn't about owning a magic crystal ball to see the future—it's about gearing up for whatever life throws at you.

I remember being a teen, just like you, lost in a sea of endless career choices, and boy, could I have used a handy guide like this. That's why I put pen to paper and wrote this book. My aim? To help you find your interests, balance your options, and pick a career path that suits you. I want to equip you with all the right gear to face whatever the future throws your way, making sure you feel confident and prepped up.

Whether you're just starting to think about your future career or already have a dream job in mind, this book is for you. It's your guide to navigating the complex world of career planning, discovering your strengths and interests, and building the skills and knowledge you need to succeed in any career you choose.

Why This Book and Why Now?

Choosing a career? Huge deal, right? Especially when you're in your teens. It's not just about finding a job; it's about finding your place, your passion, and your groove in this crazy world. That's a truckload of pressure when you're already dealing with all the rollercoaster stuff that comes with growing up.

And the pressure and confusion? Just the tip of the iceberg. The job market is changing faster than a cheetah on a sugar rush. Tech is revamping industries, conjuring up jobs we hadn't even thought of a few years ago. The global economy is more intertwined than a bowl of spaghetti, and the skills you need to make it big keep on changing. Yeah, it's a lot to swallow when you're just trying to figure out what you want to do.

Add in the unique challenges of being a teen in today's world. You're growing up in a digital age, with social media bombarding you with comparison traps and future uncertainties. You're trying to survive a school system that seems hell-bent on preparing you for college, sometimes leaving you without room to explore different career paths. And you're seeing big, gnarly problems in the world that need innovative solutions, making you wonder where you fit into the picture.

And just when we thought things were complicated enough, the pandemic waltzed in, throwing career planning into a wild spin. It's like someone picked up the globe and shook it, affecting industries and thrusting remote work into the limelight. It's been a wake-up call that adaptability is key when everything's up in the air. That's why we need a practical, down-to-earth guide to help you find your way through the foggy maze of career planning.

I get it. I remember being a teen, with a head full of questions and a heart full of doubts about the future. It was a whirlwind of stress, uncertainty, excitement, and fear all tangled up. But now, with the wisdom of adulting and mentoring other teens under my belt, I want to pass on what I've picked up along the way.

That's the whole point of this book. I'm convinced that with the right tools and some savvy guidance, you can tackle the confusing world of career planning like a boss. You can uncover what lights you up, grow your skills, and find a career that vibes with your values and dreams. You can look to the future not with fear or uncertainty, but with a spark of excitement and a glimmer of hope.

This book is here to help you make wise choices about your future. It's about giving you the reins to steer your own career planning journey, investigate your options, and craft a vision for your future that feels both satisfying and reachable. With everything that's happening in the world right now, there's no better moment to start mapping out your career.

Why Not Other Career Planning Books?

As a teen, I was on a personal mission to figure out what on earth I was supposed to do with my life. I buried my nose in loads of career planning books, hunting for answers. Now, looking back, I remember a few reasons why those books just didn't click:

1. Some were loaded with grand theories and blanket advice but fell short on handing out the practical tools or steps I needed. I was looking for something I could put into action straightaway, not just theoretical clouds drifting around in my head.

2. Others threw complicated frameworks and theories at me, which, sure, they were kind of cool, but they also felt like trying to solve a Rubik's cube

when I was just beginning to explore my career options. I needed something more straightforward, something that wouldn't give me a headache.

3. Then there were books that had solid advice, but let's be real - they were about as exciting as watching paint dry. I'd read them, get a jolt of inspiration that fizzled out faster than a cheap sparkler, and forget all about them a week later. None of that advice really stuck or gave me the push I needed to take action.

Now, don't get me wrong. There are some top-notch career planning books out there that are worth their weight in gold. But, I noticed a missing puzzle piece.

When I decided to spill what I've learned about career planning, I knew I wanted to flip the script. No lofty concepts or overloading you with theories here. I wanted to give you tangible, hands-on strategies that actually helped me find my own way. And most importantly, I wanted to dish it out in a way that's intriguing, easy to digest, and laser-focused on you – the up-and-coming generation gearing up to rock the world.

So, here's the deal. This book is meant to be your friendly guide, penned by someone who's walked a mile in your shoes. I'm not here to dictate what career you should chase, but I'm all about equipping you with the knowledge, skills, and self-assuredness to make savvy decisions about your own future.

Making the Most Out of This Book

Picture this book as your go-to manual or your trusty GPS steering you towards an awesome and fulfilling career. It's split into two main chunks.

First off, we dive into 'Crafting Your Career Game Plan'. This bit is all about getting up close and personal with you - what lights your fire, what you're a natural at, and what gets you buzzing with excitement. Once we've nailed that down, we're gonna help you pair these up with jobs that might just be your dream come true. We'll also help you draft a crystal-clear, action-packed blueprint for your career.

Here's what your career planning roadmap looks like:

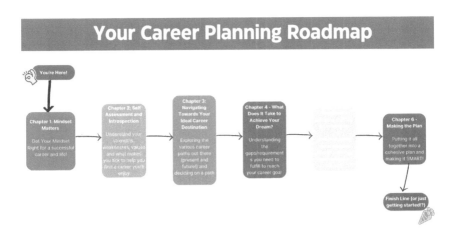

Next up in part 2, we have 'Bringing the Plan to Life - Essential Skills to Smash Your Career Goal'. This is where we'll equip you with the know-how and hacks to bring your career plan to life. You'll find chapters on crafting a standout resume, the magic of networking, how to nail job interviews, and even a sneak peek into the worlds of freelancing and entrepreneurship. We'll dish out real, hands-on advice to get you ready to take on the working world.

As you flip through the book, take a second to mull over what you're soaking up, scribble down notes, and give the exercises and activities in each chapter a try. These aren't just for kicks - they're designed to help you really grasp and put into practice everything we're chewing over.

This book isn't meant to be a one-hit-wonder. It's like your favorite game guide or cheat sheet you can flip back to whenever you need a hand.

Whether you're still juggling school or starting to wade into the job pool, this book is here to hand you the tools, insider tips, and confidence to turn your career plan into the real deal. We can't wait to cheer you on as you conquer amazing things!

Remember, the future's in your hands. So, let's hit the ground running and start carving out your dream career today!

I

Crafting Your Career Game Plan

Chapter 1 - Your Mindset Matters

"Your attitude, not your aptitude, will determine your altitude." – Zig Ziglar

E very morning you wake up with a choice. The choice to let the day's challenges control you, or the choice to take control of your own destiny. Navigating your career journey can seem overwhelming, but without the right mindset, the tides will never turn in your favor. So let's start our shared adventure by exploring the cornerstone of success: your mindset.

You have the power to shape your future

As a teenager, you're at a super important point in your life where the decisions you make can seriously impact your future. By adopting a proactive mindset and taking responsibility for your choices, you can set yourself on a path toward an awesome and successful career. So, always remember that your future is in your hands, and you can take the necessary steps to shape it according to your dreams and aspirations.

Life can feel like a roller coaster sometimes, right? With so much going on, it's easy to get caught up in just reacting to whatever's happening around you.

A reactive mindset is like being on autopilot, where you're always responding to stuff without really taking control of your actions or decisions. Sure, it might get you through the day, but in the long run, you'll probably end up feeling overwhelmed, stressed, and like you're not really in control of your life.

Take Emily, for example. She was a high school junior who felt like she was always playing catch-up with her assignments and after-school activities. Staying up late to finish homework, stressing about exams, and worrying about the future seemed like her normal routine. She was just reacting to everything happening around her instead of taking charge of her life.

Then, one day, Emily went to a workshop at her school that introduced her to the idea of a proactive mindset. She discovered that by anticipating challenges, setting goals, and taking deliberate steps to reach them, she could take back control of her life and dial down her stress levels.

Switching to a proactive mindset is all about grabbing the reins of your life and making conscious choices to shape your future. It means looking ahead, anticipating possible challenges and opportunities, setting goals, and taking purposeful action to reach them. When you adopt a proactive mindset, you'll be better prepared to handle life's ups and downs, seize opportunities that come your way, and feel more in control of your destiny. In short, you'll be empowered to create the life you want!

Over time, Emily noticed a huge difference in her life. She felt less swamped and stressed, and she even started enjoying her activities and schoolwork more. She also discovered new interests and opportunities she'd never thought of before. By making the shift from reactive to proactive, Emily took control of her life and set herself on the path to success. And you can too!

Embrace the power you have to shape your future and make the mindset shift today.

Growth Mindset, Here We Come!

You might've heard the phrase "Growth Mindset" being mentioned here and there, and maybe you've got a rough idea of what it implies, but... how about we delve deeper and truly grasp how it can help you ace life's curve balls with a positive spirit.

Ever felt like luck just doesn't seem to favor you? Like, no matter how much effort you put in, things don't seem to fall in place. Well, buckle up for a mind shift that could totally turn the tables: the growth mindset.

Imagine this: truly believing that you can develop your skills and smarts through grit, dedication, and resilience. Pretty cool right? That's what a growth mindset is all about. It's like giving yourself a pat on the back, encouraging yourself to welcome challenges, learn from slip-ups, and constantly seek ways to level up.

Let's picture a situation: Meet Alex, a 10th grader who's always had a tough time with math. He felt like it just wasn't his cup of tea. So, he'd steer clear of anything remotely challenging in math and surrender when hit with hard problems.

But then, one fine day, Alex's math teacher shared that intelligence and skills weren't set in stone at birth – they could be grown over time with effort and practice. Alex pondered, "Why not give it a try?"

So, instead of running from those daunting math problems, Alex started seeing them as opportunities to learn and grow. He sought advice from his teacher, teamed up with a study group, and even tackled math problems at home. When he tripped, he didn't throw in the towel. He dissected where he slipped and used that knowledge to sharpen his problem-solving abilities.

And guess what? Alex's growth mindset started to make waves. Math problems no longer scared him, and he quit fearing mistakes. Instead, he saw them as priceless learning opportunities that helped him get better at math. The cherry on top? This fresh mindset didn't just impact his math grades – it also influenced other areas of his life, making him more tenacious and confident in his ability to learn and evolve.

So, if you're ready to flip your viewpoint and start seeing obstacles and setbacks as chances for growth and skill enhancement, give the growth mindset a whirl. Trust me, it's a game-changer that'll help you have faith in your ability to adapt, tackle hurdles, and flourish in both your personal and professional journey.

Regardless of who you are or where you're at on this roller coaster called life, believe me, you can change. All it needs is a dash of determination to transform, loads of faith in yourself, and the readiness to dig in your heels and get down to work.

Now that you're geared up with a growth mindset and prepped to face life's challenges, let's dive into the next segment of our voyage. We'll discover ten lifelong traits that, paired with your sparkling new mindset, can set you up for a thriving career and an even more rewarding life.

10 Powerhouse Traits That'll Propel Your Career and Life to New Heights

Curiosity: Your Ultimate Superpower

You know that feeling when you just can't stop asking "Why?" or "How does that work?" That's curiosity doing its magic, and it's like having your own superpower when it comes to learning and growing as a person. Being curious is like being a detective or an explorer, always ready for the next big adventure, the next cool idea, or the next awesome opportunity. It's your secret map to finding what you love, discovering the perfect job for you, and keeping up in a world that's moving at warp speed.

So, how can you power up your curiosity? It's all about being a question-asking, knowledge-seeking ninja. Dive into books, watch fascinating documentaries, listen to mind-blowing podcasts – anything that piques your interest. Make it your mission to learn something new every single day. Try out different hobbies, join all sorts of clubs at school, or take on projects that make you step outside your comfort zone. The more curious you are, the more you'll learn about the world and yourself.

Self-awareness: Your Inner Compass to Success

Want to be a boss at making decisions and chasing your dreams? Then it's time to rev up your self-awareness! This means getting to know the real you - the good, the bad, and everything in between. Your superpowers, your weaknesses, what you stand for, and what gets you all fired up. When you're self-aware, you can pick careers that put your talents on full display and make your passions come alive. Let's say you're a chatty Cathy who lives to lend a helping hand, careers like teaching or counseling could be your perfect match. Plus, self-awareness helps you spot where you need a bit more practice, so you can keep climbing higher on your career ladder.

In chapter 2 we'll dive deep into all the ways you can introspect and understand who you are on a deeper level.

Resilience: The Secret Ingredient to Overcoming Life's Hurdles

Here's the thing: setbacks and challenges are inevitable in any career journey. That's where resilience comes in! This powerful trait enables you to bounce back and conquer obstacles like a champ. Whether it's rejection, failure, or unexpected twists and turns, being resilient helps you learn from these experiences and come back even stronger. For instance, if you miss out on your dream internship, use that experience to fine-tune your application strategy and prepare for future opportunities. By cultivating resilience, you'll stay motivated and committed to achieving your career goals, no matter the hurdles.

Think of resilience as a muscle—the more you flex it, the stronger it becomes. Start by setting realistic goals and breaking them down into smaller, achievable steps. Embrace setbacks and failures as chances to grow and level up. Use positive self-talk and remember your achievements, especially during tough times. Surround yourself with a supportive squad that cheers you on and believes in your potential. And hey, don't be afraid to ask for help when needed. Building resilience takes time, but the payoff is absolutely worth it.

Open-Mindedness: Embrace a World of Possibilities and Uncover Hidden Gems

Open-mindedness is like having a magic key that can unlock doors to loads of different ideas, viewpoints, and experiences. It's super handy when you're looking at all the possible career paths out there. By being open-minded, you can check out a whole bunch of different options. Like, you might think finance is all about being a number-crunching wizard. But if you're open to it, you'll see it's also about solving tricky problems, flexing your creative muscles, and being a team player – stuff that might actually get you excited. By keeping your mind open, you'll find cool opportunities you didn't even know were there and supercharge your career journey.

So, how do you become more open-minded? Jump into all sorts of experiences and points of view. Read books or watch movies that make you question what you believe, go to cultural festivals or workshops, or chat with people who come from different walks of life or see things differently than you. Keep working on your listening skills and being empathetic, trying to understand where others are coming from without jumping to conclusions. The more open-minded you are, the more you'll learn and thrive.

Adaptability: The Key to Thriving in a Dynamic World

Adaptability is all about rolling with the punches and thriving in fresh situations or changing surroundings. It's important because industries keep evolving and the job market's always on the move. Let's say robots start doing parts of the job you're eyeing (it's happening as you read this!). You'll need to get your adaptability game on by learning new skills or even considering different career paths. By becoming a pro at adapting, you'll be ready to handle whatever the job market throws at you and set yourself up for a rock-solid career.

So, how do you become more adaptable? Stay in the loop with the latest trends and breakthroughs in stuff you're interested in, so you can see changes coming and get ready for them. Boost your problem-solving skills by tackling challenges head-on and brainstorming clever fixes. Learn to stay cool under pressure and handle tough situations with a go-with-the-flow attitude and open mind. The more adaptable you are, the better you'll be at handling whatever surprises life has in store.

Proactivity: Seize the Initiative and Shape Your Destiny

Think of proactivity like this - it's all about grabbing the wheel and steering your own life, instead of just waiting for things to happen. When you're proactive, you supercharge your career journey and get to call the shots for your future. Say there's an industry that really catches your eye. Why not reach out to pros in the field for a chat or join industry events to grow your network and know-how? When you're proactive in planning your career, you're always one step ahead and way more likely to turn your dreams into reality.

So, how do you boost your proactivity? Start by setting clear goals and sketching out a game plan to hit them (if you're reading this, chances are you're more proactive than your peers!). Show some initiative by volunteering for projects at school or in your community, or by hunting down internships and job-shadowing chances in a field you're into. And don't be afraid to reach out to pros for advice or mentorship. Remember, the more proactive you are, the more you're in control of your own success story.

Gratitude: The Secret Ingredient to a Fulfilled and Successful Life

Gratitude is all about savoring the good stuff in life and giving props to the people who make a difference. When you're grateful, you're happier, your mind's healthier, and your relationships are stronger. All of this can power up your career big time. Like, saying "thank you" to your mentors or work buddies for their help can make your ties stronger and your workspace a whole lot friendlier.

So, how do you get your gratitude game on point? Try starting a gratitude journal and jot down three things you're thankful for each day. This simple habit can help you see the glass as half full, not half empty, and notice all the good stuff you've already got going on. Make it a habit to say "thanks" to people, whether that's with a quick "thank you," a heartfelt letter, or a small gift. As you grow your gratitude attitude, you'll see both your personal and work life getting a serious boost.

Humility: The Foundation of Genuine Growth and Success

Humility is all about realizing you've got stuff to learn and respect what others know and can do (no matter what stage you're at in this journey of life!). When you're humble, you're better at learning from goof-ups, asking for help, and teaming up with others for mega wins in your career. Like, admitting you don't have all the answers and asking for a helping hand can score you some game-changing advice and chances to level up.

So, how do you get your humility game strong? Remind yourself that nobody's perfect and it's totally cool not to have all the answers. Be open to feedback and take any criticism as a chance to learn and do better. Celebrate other people's wins and give credit where it's due. By keeping it humble, you'll build super strong relationships, create awesome team vibes, and in the end, become a more successful and well-rounded pro.

Responsibility: Unlock the Power of Owning Your Actions and Choices

By being responsible, you claim your choices, you get to hold the reins of your life and career, and that means you can steer yourself toward winning. For instance, if you're having a tough time in a class, being responsible means owning up to your part in the struggle and finding ways to bump up your game.

So, how do you become more responsible? Start by checking out your actions and what were their results and consequences. Are you truly giving it your all to hit your goals, or are there spots where you could crank up the effort? If things don't pan out as you hoped, dodge the blame game with others or external factors, and instead, ask yourself what lessons **you** can snag from the experience. Stay true to your commitments and keep your promises, whether it's finishing a project on time or helping out a buddy in a jam.

Accountability: Crank Up Your Power by Owning Your Moves

Accountability is like a sibling to responsibility. It's all about standing up for your actions, choices, and whatever happens because of them. When you wrap your arms around accountability, you're telling the world you're dead serious about your goals and you're all-in to make things roll. For instance, if you told your team you'd wrap up your part of the project on time, it's on you to make it happen. By being accountable, you build trust, earn props from others, and set yourself up to score big in your career and life.

So, how do you become more accountable? Start by setting clear expectations for yourself and others – make sure everyone's on the same wavelength about what needs to get done and by when. If stuff changes or if you need a hand, talk it out openly and honestly, but dodge the excuse game. Use your slip-ups as stepping stones to grow and get better.

Remember, no one's perfect – we all stumble every now and then. But the secret to boosting accountability is admitting those trips and figuring out how to fix things. When you own your actions and stick to your commitments, you'll unlock your potential and pave a path for a successful, rewarding career and life.

Now, you might be thinking that responsibility and accountability sound like twins, and yeah, it can get pretty confusing (believe me, I was scratching my head over this when I was a teen!). Both responsibility and accountability are two key skills you need as you grow up and start flying solo.

Responsibility is like that little voice in your head that nudges you about stuff you're supposed to do, like cramming for a test or helping out with chores at home. It's about getting and owning the tasks thrown your way and making sure you see them through.

Accountability, on the flip side, is all about owning the fallout of your actions. When you nail something, you take the credit for it and feel stoked about what you've achieved. But if you drop the ball or don't meet the bar, accountability is about fessing up to your blunders, learning from them, and figuring out how to up your game next time.

So, responsibility is about being clued into your duties and knocking them out, while accountability is about being straight with yourself and others about what comes out of your actions, whether they're awesome or not so much.

Setting Realistic Expectations for Career Success

Before we jump to the next part, let's get real about something majorly important: setting realistic expectations for your career dreams. I know, it's super tempting to aim for the moon and score those big, shiny dreams ASAP. But, wait up! We gotta do a little reality check. Success isn't a fast-track thing – it needs time, sweat, and yep, sometimes a few roadblocks. So let's talk about how to handle those big dreams and understand that real success is all about baby steps and sticking with it.

First things first: let's get serious about your goals. While it's totally cool to have big dreams, it's also key to remember that no one starts at the finish line. Seriously, even the biggest success stories had to start somewhere. So, when making your career goals, make sure they're doable and reachable. Think of it like leveling up in a video game – you gotta pass one level at a time. Set smaller, achievable targets that'll keep you pumped and moving forward. Did you know, Oprah started her career as a local news reporter? Yep, even someone as big as Oprah didn't just warp to the top; she had to level up, facing challenges and setbacks along the way.

You have to learn to enjoy the journey. Because that's what your career is: a journey filled with twists, turns, and surprise levels. And guess what? That's totally okay! In fact, it's kinda the point. Your career path isn't going to be a straight shot, and that's what makes it an epic adventure. So, learn to roll with the punches.

Now, let's talk about sticking with it. Because trust me, success doesn't happen without it. You're going to face challenges, and even failures along the way. But the key is to learn from those experiences and keep pushing forward. Remember, every loss you get brings you one step closer to a win. So, stay determined, stay focused, and never quit your dreams.

Lastly, don't forget to celebrate your victories – no matter how small. Seriously, give yourself a high five for every target you hit, because you earned it! Celebrating your progress will keep you pumped and remind you that you're on the right track.

Dream big but remember it takes time, consistency, and patience to get there. The journey will be all the more fun and enjoyable.

So, now that we're all set with the right mindset for scoring those wins, let's jump into the next chapter. We'll check out how knowing yourself better can help you make solid choices and pick the perfect career path that goes with your unique skills and passions. Strap in for a journey of self-discovery!

Chapter 2 - Self-Assessment and Introspection

"Your vision will become clear only when you can look into your own heart. Who looks outside, dreams; who looks inside, awakes." – Carl Jung

As we set sail on this journey of career planning, it's time for a little heart-to-heart. You see, before we can start plotting a course for your dreams, we need to know where we're starting from. As Maya Angelou once said, "You can't know where you're going until you know where you've been." That's why this chapter is all about introspection and self-assessment, the dynamic duo that'll be our compass and map as we chart your course to career success.

Picture yourself as the captain of your own life-ship, ready to embark on a thrilling voyage toward your future. Now, any seasoned sailor will tell you that before you can navigate the choppy seas and skirt around treacherous reefs, you've got to know your current coordinates. Similarly, introspection (looking inward) and self-assessment (analyzing your strengths and areas for growth) help you pinpoint your starting point and guide your journey, ensuring you can steer your ship confidently toward your dreams.

I know, I know. You might be thinking, "But I'm just a teen. How am I supposed to know what I want from my career?" Trust me, I totally get it. The pressure to pick the 'right' career path can feel overwhelming. But that's where introspection and self-assessment come to the rescue. They help you understand your passions, values, and skills, and provide the insights you need to make confident decisions about your future.

As you journey through this chapter, you'll get to know yourself on a deeper level, uncovering the unique strengths and passions that make you, well, you. This newfound self-knowledge will be your rock-solid foundation, supporting you as you build your career plan. And remember, introspection isn't a one-and-done deal. It's an ongoing process, a lifelong skill that'll help you stay true to yourself, no matter where your career journey takes you. So, let's get started, shall we?

Navigating the Self-Assessment Process: Essential Discoveries to Guide Your Career Path

Let's go on a treasure hunt of self-understanding! We're going to explore the unique traits that define you. These are the key insights you should look for in the self-assessment process to understand which careers might suit you best:

1. Your Strengths and Weaknesses: Just like your favorite superheroes, you've got strengths and weaknesses, and figuring them out is essential. We're aiming for a career where you can flex those strengths. And those weaknesses? Well, we'll find ways to work around them or even turn them into strengths.

2. Skills: Take a look at the talents you've already got in your bag. Are you the one your friends call for tech help? Maybe you're a communication whiz? Or do you naturally step up and lead? Pinning down your skills is a big part of the self-discovery puzzle.

3. Life Goals: Let your imagination run wild. What's your ultimate life goal, and where does your dream job fit into that? This isn't just about attaching a job title to your future self, it's about understanding how work fits into your life's big picture.

4. Money Matters: Sure, we all dream of big bucks. But let's get real about the lifestyle you want and how much it's going to cost. Now's the time to sketch out your financial goals before you start checking out potential salaries.

5. Personality: Are you a total extrovert or more of a behind-the-scenes person? Your personality can influence how you gel with different work environments and tasks. Recognizing these traits can help you spot where you'll shine and what work will get you excited to start your day.

6. Passions: Whether you're a gaming guru, a lover of the arts, or a tech nerd, your interests could point the way to your future job. When you love what you do, you're more likely to stay engaged and motivated. So, think about what lights you up, not just what you're good at.

7. Values: Your values are like your inner GPS. They guide your decisions and define your actions. Figuring out what you hold dear will help you pick a career that aligns with your beliefs, leading to a more satisfying and meaningful work-life.

By exploring these pieces of your personal puzzle, you're setting yourself up to win at career planning. The better you know yourself, the easier it is to find a career that clicks with who you are. You're not just picking a job, you're choosing a lifestyle, a purpose, a direction.

In the next section, we're going to spill the beans on some strategies and tools to navigate this journey of self-discovery. This is where you start plotting your course toward a career that brings you real satisfaction and success.

Exploring Your Inner World: 4 Fantastic Methods for Self-Discovery

Now that you know what to look for in the self-discovery process, we're going to explore the 4 best ways to find those insights. Ready? Let's go...

Ask yourself!

Alright, first off, let's get ready for some heart-to-heart chat with the numero uno – you! It's time to hit yourself with some real questions and dare to be truthful with your answers. Sounds intimidating? Don't fret. It's just a tête-à-tête between you and your thoughts. You're the world's best authority on yourself, and this is your opportunity to dig into the layers that make you, you.

How about we begin with a little thing called journaling? It might sound like something from a bygone era, but trust me, it's like having a secret chat with yourself, and it's a game-changer. It's like having your personalized guide to your brain, and it's seriously epic.

Now, while you're getting your thoughts down on paper, spare a moment to travel back in time. Reflect on your wins, your losses, and everything in between. Ask yourself, "What wisdom did I gain? How have these experiences sculpted me?" This isn't about getting stuck in the past, but rather understanding how it's crafted the incredible person you are today.

And don't just stop at the past. Let your mind wander to the future as well.

Paint pictures of different scenarios – where do you see yourself in 5 years? 10 years? How does your dream day look like? Imagining these scenarios can offer great insight into your deepest desires and values.

Feeling a bit unsure about what to journal? No biggie. Here are some prompts to kickstart those creative cogs:

- What gets me pumped? What activities make me feel invincible?
- When have I felt like I've won the world? What was happening, and what can I learn from it?
- What challenges have come my way, and how did I tackle them? What wisdom did I gather from the process?
- What are the things I absolutely can't compromise in life? What values are closest to my heart, and how do they steer my decisions?
- How would I describe my character? How does this influence the way I interact with others and the world around me?

We've got a bigger list of questions to get your journaling rhythm on in the resources chapter at the end!

These queries (and any others that come up) will help you gain a clearer picture of who you truly are, what charges your battery, and what you desire from your career. Remember, this self-reflection journey isn't a one-and-done thing. Keep up with your journaling, keep digging into your thoughts and emotions, and see how it revolutionizes your understanding of yourself. Trust me, it'll be worth every second!

Ask People Who See You in Action

I get it, it might feel a bit strange, to ask people their thoughts about you. But believe me, it's like hitting a treasure trove of info that can seriously help you get a grip on your strengths, weaknesses, your personality style, and values that drive you. So, let's dig into why this is a big deal and how you can ace this stage.

You might be wondering, "Wait a minute, why do I need to ask other people about me? I mean, I'm with myself all day, every day, isn't there a 'know thyself' thing?" And you're not wrong, not entirely. *But here's the twist: others can sometimes spot things about us that we might miss.* They can toss us some real gems of insights that can help us step up our game, both in our personal lives and in our future careers.

Here are the people who see you day in and out and might have some insight and perspective to improve your self-understanding.

Parents

Your parents have known you since you were in diapers. They've had front-row seats to your whole life show, so their take on your journey is like solid gold. They can give you the lowdown on your strengths, the stuff you could do better, and what fires you up.

Here's what you could ask them:

- How have you seen my interests and passions shift and grow as I've gotten older?
- Can you think of times when I totally nailed something or, not so much?
- How do you reckon our family values and the way I was brought up have

shaped who I am today?

- Can you give me some examples of when I showed some serious leader-ship, problem-solving, or teamwork chops?
- Are there any skills or talents you've spotted in me that I might not even realize I have?
- Have you noticed any habits or patterns that might give a hint about my future career choices or work style?
- What stuff have you seen me get really into or super excited about?
- If you had to describe my personality, what would you say? And how do you think it could steer my career choices?
- Have you seen any changes in what I care about or what I'm interested in as I've grown up?

Parents, if you're reading this, think about these questions and get ready to have a chat with your teens!

Teachers

Your teachers have seen you tackle everything from algebra to zebra dis-section (well, hopefully not the latter!). Your teachers can serve up some insights about your intellectual strengths, potential areas of improvement, and your work style. Plus, they can clue you in on the subjects that got your gears turning and how your unique way of learning might sway your career choices. Here are some questions to help you strike gold:

- What skills or talents do you think I've got that could be a real game-changer in my future career?
- Have there been any subjects or projects in which you have seen me excel or be really challenged?
- In what ways do you think my learning style and classroom behavior could shape my career choices?
- Do you remember any times when I totally killed it at problem-solving,

communication, or teamwork?
- Are there any particular study areas or skills you think I should be leveling up to get a head start on my future career?
- Based on my grades and interests, what career paths do you think could be a good fit for me?
- Have you noticed any changes in my motivation, interests, or strengths during my time in your class?
- How do you think my performance in your subject might give me a hint about my potential career direction?

Teachers, help your students unlock their potential and get a head start on their future careers.

Guidance Counselors

Guidance counselors are trained to help you plan your future, so why not pick their brains about potential career paths that suit your personality and interests? They can also suggest resources and programs at school to help you explore further. Here are a couple of questions you could ask them:

- Based on our interactions and my academic performance, what careers do you think might be a good fit for me?
- Are there any resources or programs at school that you recommend for exploring my career interests further?
- How can I make the most of my remaining time in high school to prepare for my future career?
- Can you recommend any clubs, extracurricular activities, or volunteer opportunities that align with my interests and career goals?
- What steps should I take to better understand my strengths, weaknesses, and values as they relate to my career aspirations?
- How can I develop a strong support network to help me succeed in my future career?

- What resources are available to help me research potential colleges or vocational programs that align with my career goals?

By asking your guidance counselor these questions, you can gain valuable insights for your future career exploration, ensuring you're well-prepared for the next chapter of your life.

Coaches

Your coaches have a front-row seat to your teamwork, leadership, and problem-solving skills. They've seen you tackle challenges, make tough decisions, and put your all into your passion. So, why not find out what they think could make you shine in your future career and what you could work on to level up your game? Let's break it down with these guiding questions:

- What strengths have you seen me display as a teammate or leader?
- How do you think my experiences in sports or extracurricular activities could score me some points in my future career?
- Are there any habits or traits that you think I should level up to be a superstar in my chosen field?
- Can you recall any times when I've shown resilience or adaptability?
- How have you seen me react to curveballs or challenges, and what can I learn from these experiences to up my game?
- In what ways have I demonstrated communication or collaboration with my teammates, and how could these skills play out in a professional setting?
- Are there any specific roles or responsibilities I've taken on within the team that might be a sneak peek of my future career interests?
- How can I continue to level up my leadership skills and personal growth outside of sports or extracurricular activities?
- Based on your experience with other athletes or performers, are there any career paths you think I should explore, given my unique strengths

and interests?
- Can you recommend any resources or strategies for further developing the skills and qualities I've shown in our team setting?

Coaches, share your insights and help your students navigate the complex world of career planning. They'll appreciate your guidance!

Friends and Siblings

Your buddies have seen you in all sorts of social situations and know what you're like when you're just hanging out. You might not think so, but they can actually offer some real insights into your interpersonal skills and how you interact with others. So, ask them about your best qualities, the experiences you've enjoyed together, and any challenges you've faced.

- What do you think are my best qualities as a friend or brother/sister, and how might they translate to a professional setting?
- What are some activities or experiences we've shared that you think I've enjoyed the most?
- Have you noticed any patterns in the types of challenges or obstacles I tend to face, and how do you think I can overcome them?
- In what ways have I demonstrated leadership or initiative in our friend group or family, and how might these skills apply to my future career?
- Can you recall any moments where I've shown empathy or understanding towards others, and how might these qualities be beneficial in a professional context?
- Are there any areas where you think I could improve my communication or collaboration skills, based on our interactions?
- How would you describe my problem-solving or decision-making abilities in various situations, and do you think these are strengths I could bring to a career?

- Based on your knowledge of my interests and hobbies, are there any career paths you think I should consider or explore further?
- Have you observed any growth or changes in me over the years that you think would be relevant to my career development?

By asking these additional questions, you'll gain valuable insights from the people who know you best in your personal life, and these perspectives can help inform your career choices and self-assessment.

Mentors

Next up, we've got the Yodas of your life, the mentors. If you're part of any clubs, organizations, or activities outside of school, the leaders in these groups can offer a galaxy of insights. We have a whole section on how to find the right mentors in the networking chapter in part 2, so don't worry if you're clueless about finding mentors.

They've seen you in different situations, maybe even doing things you've never tried before. So, let's find out what they think could be the secrets to success for your future career and what you might want to work on to be the best version of yourself. Here are some questions to guide your conversation:

- Are there any traits or habits that you think I should develop further to reach my potential in my chosen field?
- Can you recall any times when I've shown resilience, creativity, or adaptability that could serve me well in my career?
- How have you seen me respond to unfamiliar tasks or challenges, and what can I learn from these experiences?
- In what ways have I effectively collaborated or communicated with others in our group, and how could these skills be an asset in a professional setting?

- Are there any specific roles or tasks I've taken on that could hint at my future career interests?
- How can I continue to develop my leadership skills, personal growth, and interests outside of this group or activity?
- Can you suggest any resources or strategies for further honing the skills and qualities I've displayed in our group setting?

Mentors, your unique insights could be just what your mentees need to make informed decisions about their future careers!

Part-Time Employers or Internship Supervisors

Ever held a part-time job, completed an internship, or volunteered somewhere? If so, your employers or supervisors have seen you in a work environment and can offer priceless wisdom on your work ethic, skills, and interests. They've seen how you handle responsibilities, how you interact with others in a professional setting, and how you manage challenges. Here are some thought-provoking questions to ask them:

- What strengths and skills have you seen me exhibit in my role here?
- How could my experiences in this job or internship inform my future career choices?
- Are there any work habits or traits that you think I should develop further to excel in my professional life?
- Can you recall instances where I demonstrated resilience, adaptability, or creativity in the workplace?
- How have you observed me responding to work-related challenges, and what can I learn from these instances?
- In what ways have I successfully communicated or collaborated with others in this work setting, and how might these skills be relevant in a career context?

- Are there specific tasks or responsibilities I've undertaken here that could hint at my future career preferences?
- How could I continue to develop my professional skills and personal growth outside of this job or internship?
- Based on your professional experience, are there any career paths you believe I should explore, given my demonstrated strengths and interests?
- Can you recommend any resources or strategies for refining the skills and qualities I've exhibited in this work setting?

Employers and supervisors, it's time to help guide the career choices of your young workers. Your feedback can play a crucial role in shaping their professional journey, so let's get that conversation rolling!

You might've noticed there's a lot of overlap between these questions and it's that way for a reason! Collect your responses from everyone and you can compare and contrast their perspectives.

For example, your coaches get to see a side of you that your teachers don't and so they might have a different response about your strengths and abilities. You can also reflect on them based on your own responses from the journaling exercise above to understand yourself better.

In the end, gathering views from everyone gives you a clearer and complete picture of who you are.

Discover Yourself Through Assessments

There I was, scrolling through the internet, searching for answers about who I was and where I was headed. Little did I know that there were actual assessments out there designed to help me figure it all out. I mean, if you're looking for some extra insight, these tests can be a goldmine!

SAT, ACT, and Other Scholastic Assessments

Sure, SATs, ACTs, and other scholastic assessments may feel like a total drag, but let's reframe them as personal growth opportunities. Think of them as your personal 'brain gym', honing your critical thinking, problem-solving, and language skills.

These tests are like a mirror, reflecting your academic strengths and growth areas. Not only can this guide your academic journey and help tailor your course and extracurricular selections, but it can also help you make informed decisions about your future college choices.

Here's the fun part: spot patterns between your test results and your interests. For example, if you're a whizz at analytical and math problems, careers in engineering or finance could be up your alley. Or perhaps you've got a knack for languages and a passion for helping others. In that case, roles in education, social work, or counseling might be your calling.

But here's the key: remember to consider your values and interests when evaluating your results. The sweet spot for your career choice should be at the intersection of your abilities and passions.

Remember, these assessments are just snapshots of your academic abilities at a given time. *They don't determine your worth, and they definitely don't limit your potential.*

Use these scholastic assessments as a guide, helping you understand where you stand academically and pointing towards potential career paths. But always remember, it's your unique blend of strengths, weaknesses, values, interests, and traits that will shape your career journey.

Online Aptitude, Personality, and Strengths Assessments

Online assessments are like secret cheat codes in the game of self-discovery. Picture them as treasure maps, guiding you through the awesome labyrinth of your personality, values, and passions.

We've included a load of online assessments in the resources chapter of this book. Find your zen spot, free of distractions, before you start. Be real with your answers, and remember, there's no stress here. No right or wrong answers – just you being your authentic self!

Here's how to make the best use of these assessments:

Reflect and ruminate: Once you've finished an assessment, ponder the results. Do they vibe with what you know about yourself, your values, and your dreams?

Spot the similarities: Cross-reference your results from different assessments. Notice any echoes? They give you a mega-zoom view of your strengths, weaknesses, and interests. It's like your very own personality puzzle coming together.

Get others' take: Show your results to trusted pals, teachers, parents, or mentors. They might see things you've missed and give you extra insights.

Keep an open mind: Remember, these assessments are just tools. They aren't fortune tellers. Don't sweat the results too much and trust your own instincts and experiences. They're the big players in your career decision-making.

Get moving: Use your results as a launchpad for more discovery. Dive into careers that line up with your results, and talk to career counselors, mentors, or your parents about what you've found.

And remember this self-assessment process is a marathon, not a sprint. Check back on your results now and then. They're like breadcrumbs on your journey of figuring out who you are and where you're headed.

Online assessments are like handy gadgets in your self-knowing toolkit. And remember, always stay true to yourself and keep the grand scheme in mind. Your path is totally unique, and you'll find what works best for you.

By blending these assessments with your self-discovery, you'll have a sturdier platform to make savvy calls about your future.

Try New Things! Experiment!

With only a handful of years under your belt, there's a whole universe of experiences waiting for you. Sometimes, the best way to discover your strengths, interests, and values is by plunging into uncharted waters. After all, you won't know if you're good at something until you try it, right?

Engaging in experiential learning opportunities can be like holding up a mirror to your skills, preferences, and passions. It's about diving into diverse activities and unearthing what makes your heart race and your talents shine. So, where do you start?

1. **Join clubs and organizations**: Make your mark in clubs and organizations at school or within your community. Drama, art, music clubs, sports teams, volunteer groups - every new experience is a chance to learn more about yourself.

2. **Take up new hobbies**: Let your curiosity roam free. Explore painting, writing, cooking, or even learning a new instrument. You might uncover passions or talents you never knew were there, waiting to shape your career

choices.

3. **Volunteer your time**: Make a difference in your community by volunteering at local nonprofits or charities. Not only will you be contributing to a cause, but you'll also learn more about the values that motivate you.

4. **Participate in internships or job-shadowing**: Sink your teeth into internships or job-shadowing opportunities in fields that pique your interest. These experiences can give you a sneak peek into an industry, helping you gauge whether it's the right fit for your career aspirations.

5. **Take on leadership roles**: Don't shy away from leadership roles in your school or community. Whether it's being the captain of a sports team or organizing a local event, these opportunities can help you hone key skills and reveal your strengths in teamwork, communication, and problem-solving.

Remember, successful experimentation isn't just about what works. It's also about learning from what doesn't. Keep an open mind, embrace every opportunity as a learning experience, and don't be afraid to make mistakes. They're all stepping stones on your self-discovery journey.

As you continue to explore and grow, you're not only making informed decisions about your future career path but also enriching your life with invaluable knowledge and experiences.

You're on a quest to find the ultimate career for you, one that brings your skills and passions together in a joyous harmony. You know the feeling – when you're doing something you love, it doesn't even feel like work.

Also, don't forget that it's never too late to refine or learn new skills, especially if you've embraced a growth mindset. And let's face it, getting a head start does give you a leg up!

By now, you've probably noticed some natural inclinations toward certain subjects or activities. Whether you've got a knack for English and writing, a passion for math, a talent for fixing things, or the entrepreneurial spirit of a successful lemonade stand owner, you're starting to piece together the puzzle of YOU.

With newfound insights into your strengths, weaknesses, interests, values, and personality traits, you're ready to move on to the next chapter! In Chapter 3, we're going to dive headfirst into the thrilling process of exploring your aspirations and setting your career goals.

Are you ready to tap into your potential and dream up your perfect future?

Chapter 3 - Navigating Towards Your Ideal Career Destination

"The future belongs to those who believe in the beauty of their dreams."

– Eleanor Roosevelt

B y now you've journeyed deep into the realms of your aptitudes, strengths, weaknesses, and personality traits. As you embark on the next stage of your career planning voyage, it's time to cast your sights to the horizon and chart a course toward the diverse world of potential career paths that await.

In this chapter, we'll be guiding you through the exhilarating process of discovering the vast array of jobs and careers currently available. We'll begin by providing an in-depth overview of all the factors you should consider when identifying where you'd like to go.

And then we'll cover some of the best resources to help you research and identify potential career paths that align with your unique set of skills, values, and aspirations. So, hoist the sails and prepare to embark on an exciting journey of exploration and possibility in the world of careers!

Key Factors in Determining Your Career Direction

As you embark on this journey of career exploration, it's important to consider several key factors that will help guide your decision-making process. These factors build upon what you've discovered about yourself in Chapter 2 and help you align your unique characteristics with potential career paths.

Essential Skills and Proficiencies

Recall the strengths and weaknesses you identified in Chapter 2? This is where they come into play. When exploring potential careers, it's crucial to consider your existing skills and proficiencies. Do you have strong technical skills in a particular area, such as technology or science? Are you a natural communicator, able to connect and engage with people effortlessly? Your inherent strengths can guide you towards careers where these skills are highly valued.

However, remember that you're not limited by the skills you have now. As a young person, you're in an optimal position to learn and develop new skills that align with your interests and career aspirations. So, don't be afraid to consider careers that require skills you're eager to acquire.

Reflect on the following questions:

- What are the technical skills I already possess that I enjoy using?
- What new skills am I interested in acquiring, and which ones do I believe I could excel at with practice and learning?
- In terms of soft skills (like communication, teamwork, and problem-solving), which ones do I have, and how can I apply them in a professional context?

35

- How can I leverage these skills to carve out a rewarding career path?

Be sure to refer to the journaling prompts in the resources section! By aligning your skills and proficiencies with your career direction, you can find a path that not only suits your talents but is also fulfilling and enjoyable.

Core Values

Think of your values as your personal rule book, the ones that sit snugly in your heart, shaping your worldview, decisions, and interactions. These rooted values that you dug up in Chapter 2? They can be your secret weapon in steering you toward a career that feels genuinely meaningful and in sync with who you are.

Contemplate the following questions:

- How can my professional life be a reflection of my guiding principles?
- How can these principles fuel my professional success and personal fulfillment?
- How might my values sculpt my long-term career goals?
- Are there specific sectors or industries that align more closely with my guiding principles?
- What kind of organizational culture would harmonize with my values and promote growth?
- How can I allow my values to steer me in making informed career decisions?

Your Ideal Work Environment

Visualize this - a place where you're at your productive best, where motivation is high, and satisfaction is the order of the day. Crucial, isn't it? Especially when you're trying to pick a career that will not only make you successful but also keep you happy. And this work setting isn't just about the physicality of a place - it's about the culture, the vibe, the work style. It's about the values that the place stands for. Here's what you should consider when thinking about your ideal work environment.

Work Culture and Style: Workplaces are as diverse as they come, each boasting its unique culture and style. There are places that are team-centric and thrive on constant collaboration. Then there are those that value individual work and autonomy. Some workplaces buzz with a fast-paced, high-stakes environment, while others adopt a chill and laid-back approach. You gotta think about what kind of work culture and style aligns with your personality and work habits. Do you see yourself thriving in a structured, conventional setting? Or does a dynamic, innovative setting get your creative juices flowing?

Flexibility: With the job market constantly changing, flexibility is becoming increasingly important. This could mean having flexible work hours, the freedom to work from home, or the liberty to manage your projects. Think about how much flexibility you need in your work schedule and environment. Do you need a set schedule, or do you need flexibility to juggle other aspects of your life?

Physical Setting: While some people thrive in the buzz of a city-based office, others might do their best work in a quiet, rural setting, or even the comfort of their own home. Give some thought to your preference in terms of physical workspace.

Here are a few questions to help you brainstorm and understand your work environment preferences:

- Do I work better alone or as part of a team?
- Do I love a fast-paced, dynamic environment or a slow-paced, steady one?
- How important is flexibility in my work schedule? Do I need the ability to work from home or work unconventional hours?
- What kind of physical setting makes me feel at home and boosts my productivity?
- What are my feelings about commuting? Would I be willing to relocate for work?

Figuring out your ideal work environment can be a game-changer. It can not only help you zoom in on your job search but also increase the odds of long-term job satisfaction and success. Quite simply, it'll be a place where you'll love to work, day in and day out.

Education and Training Requirements

Alright, so as we're peeking into different jobs, it's super important to understand the education and training that comes with each. Different gigs need different levels of education, training, and certifications, and this can really help you choose your future path.

Academic Qualifications: Lots of jobs need a certain level of school education. This could be everything from finishing high school to getting a bachelor's degree, or even going all the way to get a master's or PhD for some really specialized jobs. Now, think about this - are you cool with spending four years (or maybe more) in university? Or do you dig a job that needs less school stuff but more hands-on training?

Training and Certificates: Apart from school, some jobs need specific training or certificates. This could be learning on the job for a trade job, a coding boot camp for tech wizards, or a teaching certificate for those who want to shape young minds. These can give you hands-on experience and make you stand out when you're job hunting. Are you up for that?

Time and Money: Higher education and certificates can cost a ton and take a lot of time. You gotta think about whether the money and happiness you'll get from your chosen job are worth the time and money you'll spend on getting there.

Requirements of Continuous Learning: Also, think about whether you're excited about always learning and getting better in your job. Are you up for jobs that need you to keep learning and adapting to new stuff, or do you prefer jobs that don't change much?

Here are some questions to get you thinking:

- What's the minimum academic qualification needed for my dream job? Am I ready and able to do that?
- Are there any extra training or certificates I need to be awesome in this job? Am I good with putting in the time and effort to get these?
- Considering the cost of education and training, does the money and job satisfaction seem worth it?
- Am I excited about always learning and getting better? Would I be happy in a job that needs me to keep learning?

Knowing the education and training needed for your dream job can help you make good decisions about your future. It's about matching what you dream of doing with what's really needed, making sure you're happy and able to do what it takes to get there.

Interests and Passions

What if we told you that your favorite pastime could turn into your full-time job? When you're fired up about your job because it aligns with your hobbies or interests, work feels more like play. You'll stay pumped, enjoy what you do, and totally crush it in your career.

Here are some questions you can ask yourself to brainstorm which of your interests and passions you could turn into a career:

- What hobbies or topics get my energy levels soaring?
- Can I see any themes or recurring patterns in the things that I'm totally into?
- Is there a way to link these passions to possible career paths? Are there any jobs out there that let me do what I love?
- Could I blend a few of my interests into one amazing career? What would that look like?
- Do I know someone who's turned their passion into their paycheck? What can I take away from their journey?

Remember, work doesn't have to be a snoozefest! Pick a career that sparks your interest, and you'll be setting yourself up for a fulfilling and thrilling professional journey. So, dare to dream big and let your interests light the way to your future career.

Career Progression, Growth Opportunities, and Job Market Trends

Alright, so you're getting a pretty neat picture of your future career. Hold on though! Have you given thought to your prospects for advancing in that role, the opportunities for growth and learning, and the current job market trends? Trust us, this stuff is key—it can impact your long-term job satisfaction, job security, and your professional development.

Climbing the Ladder or Hopping Around?: Different careers have different ways to level up. Some jobs have a clear hierarchy and set promotion paths, while others offer a more dynamic structure where you can hop around and pick up varied skills. You gotta decide what vibes with you. Do you prefer a role with a predictable path to the top, or are you more drawn to a job that offers a chance to dip your toes in different waters?

For example, in the field of accounting, you can start as an entry-level accountant and work your way up to roles like senior accountant, controller, or even CFO. On the other hand, there are careers that offer a more dynamic structure where you can hop around and pick up varied skills. For instance, in the world of entrepreneurship, you might start your own business and have the freedom to explore different areas of interest, from marketing to product development. It's like being a jack-of-all-trades, constantly learning and adapting.

Checking the Job Temperature: Along with your personal preferences, you'll need to keep an eye on the pulse of your chosen industry. Some careers are booming right now, boasting plenty of opportunities and job security, while others may be more of a tough grind. Look into the current and projected demand for the roles that pique your interest.

Here are some questions to help you reflect:

- What's the typical progression route in the job I'm eyeing? Does it align with my career aspirations?
- Are there opportunities for continuous learning and growth in this role?
- What's the current climate in the job market for this profession? Are there ample opportunities, or is it a bit stagnant?
- How might future trends and innovations impact this job?

Grasping how you can progress in a role and what's buzzing in the job market can help you make an informed decision about your career path. It's all about aligning your career dreams with the realities of the job market, ensuring that you're investing your energy into a career that's both fulfilling and future-proof.

Salary and Compensation

Let's talk about money! While it's not the only thing that matters, it's important to consider when choosing a career. You want to make sure your future job can support the awesome life you're dreaming of, right? So, let's break it down and dive into salary and compensation!

To get a handle on your financial goals, ask yourself these questions:

- What do I need and expect financially for the future? (Think about things like housing, travel, hobbies, and more!)
- What benefits are super important to me? Things like health insurance, retirement plans, or cool perks?
- How does my dream salary compare to the average pay for the careers I'm interested in? Is it realistic, or should I adjust my expectations?
- Am I willing to make sacrifices in other areas (like work-life balance

or job satisfaction) for a higher salary? Or do other aspects of a career matter more to me?

- How much do job stability and security matter to me when considering different careers?

It's all about finding that perfect balance between making a good living and loving what you do. So, as you explore potential careers, keep your financial expectations in mind. You're on your way to finding the perfect fit!

Lifestyle and Geographic Location

The world is your oyster, but where do you want to plant your roots and build your career? Deciding on the perfect location for your work and life is a crucial piece of the puzzle. Whether you dream of big-city living or a cozy countryside haven, there's a spot out there that's just right for you. So let's dig into some questions to help you figure out your ideal location and how it fits into the grand scheme of things:

- What's my preferred living and working environment - urban, rural, or perhaps overseas?
- What factors influence my location choice? (Consider aspects like climate, cost of living, and closeness to loved ones)
- Are certain industries or job markets prominent in the locations I'm interested in?
- How does my desired lifestyle (social scene, outdoor pursuits, cultural activities) mesh with my potential locations?
- Am I open to relocation for a job, or would I rather stay near my current home base?
- What type of work-life balance am I seeking? (Options could range from

flexible hours, and remote work, to a traditional office setting)
- How crucial are job stability and security for me? (Am I inclined towards a riskier, potentially high-yielding career, or would I prefer a steadier profession?)

Once you know your preferred location, desired work-life balance, and job stability preferences you can start researching the job market and industries in that area. It's all about finding the perfect balance between a satisfying career and a fulfilling lifestyle.

Your Goals and Purpose

It's now time to take a step back and gaze into the future. We're talking about the big picture, the long haul, the grand vision of your life! Yup, we're diving into the realm of goals and purpose. Your career choices should align with what you want to achieve in life and how you want to make a difference. Discovering the right career is like completing a masterpiece puzzle with the perfect piece.

So, let's dive into some thought-provoking questions to help you connect your career choices to your goals and purpose:

- What are my ultimate personal and professional goals in life? (Be specific and dream big!)
- How do my career choices connect with my life's purpose and mission? (Think about the impact you want to have in your life and in the world.)
- Are there any milestones or achievements I want to reach in my chosen career path? (These could be promotions, awards, or even starting your own business!)

- How can I break down my long-term goals into smaller, more manageable steps? (Create a roadmap to success by setting short-term goals and tracking your progress.)
- What resources or support do I need to reach my goals in my chosen career? (Think about mentors, networking opportunities, or professional development.)

By reflecting on these questions, you'll not only create a vision for your future but also gain clarity on how your career choices align with your overall life goals and purpose. Remember, your career is more than just a job – it's an essential part of your life's journey. So, dream big, stay true to your purpose, and get ready to conquer the world, one goal at a time!

Now that we've laid it all out, it's time for some introspection. Don't worry, though! It's all part of the journey. Take it one step at a time, and you'll find the career that's right for you. And remember, it's okay to change your mind. Life is full of twists and turns, and your career might lead you somewhere entirely unexpected. So, stay open to the possibilities and enjoy the journey!

First Find Out Where You Don't Want to Go!

So, there are like a zillion different career paths out there. Yeah, it can feel kind of dizzying with all those choices, right? Before we start chasing down the awesome stuff you're all about, let's do a big favor for Future You and sort out what you DON'T want in a job. This way, you won't get stuck in career quicksand, making your whole dream job quest way less stressful.

Figuring out what you don't want in a job is super important, and here's why:

You Get Crystal Clear: When you know what you're not into, it's like solving a puzzle. You start seeing the pieces that DO fit and get a clearer picture of your dream job.

You Save Time: Who wants to scroll through every job out there? Not you! By knowing what you don't want, you can zero in on the jobs that actually get you excited.

Avoid disappointment: Picture this - you're stuck in a job that totally isn't you. No thanks! By knowing what you don't want, you can dodge those career choices that you'd regret later.

Here are some questions to think about to help you figure out your job no-gos:

- What tasks or activities totally bore you to tears?
- Are there certain work environments where you just can't see yourself?
- Do you like flying solo or are you more of a team player?
- Are there any industries or sectors you're just not feeling?
- What work values do you totally not vibe with?
- Are there skills you just don't enjoy using or don't want to rely on in your job?
- Do you have lifestyle preferences or commitments that you want to factor into your career thoughts? Like, are you all about work-life balance or have family matters to consider?
- Are there career paths you've looked into or heard about that just don't jive with your passions or long-term goals?
- Have you had any jobs or volunteer experiences where you were like, "Nope, not for me?" What didn't you like about those gigs?

Remember, these questions are just to get you started. Take your time to think about each one and write down your ideas. This will help you get a clear vision of your dream job and make your career search way easier.

Alright! Now that we've sorted out the stuff you're not into, let's flip the script and dig into what you DO want! Up next, we've got a bunch of cool tools and resources to help you get to know different jobs and make your dream job hunt a fun and exciting adventure.

A Guide to Discovering Current Job Options

Okay, let's face it. Trying to take stock of all the jobs that exist is kinda like trying to count all the stars in the sky or emojis on your phone—it seems virtually impossible, right? No worries, I've got you covered. I'm about to share some of the best resources that'll help you get a grip on this whole 'what-jobs-are-out-there' conundrum.

Your Guidance/Career Counselor

Your first pit stop on this adventure is probably way closer than you think - your school's career counselor. They're loaded with intel about career fairs, internships, and workshops. Plus, they can help you take a closer look at specific industries, find nifty job shadowing opportunities, and even connect you with people who've already chased down careers you're interested in. So don't play hard to get, reach out to them and ask for a hand - it's literally what they're there for!

The Internet

Don't underestimate the power of the internet when you're hunting down career info. The internet is a treasure trove of information when it comes to researching careers. For example, the Bureau of Labor Statistics' Occupational Outlook Handbook and O*NET OnLine are like virtual treasure chests of career data. These sites are great starting points for your job exploration journey. And, for a bigger list of websites to check out, don't forget to sneak a peek at the resources chapter in this book.

Your Local or School Library

Your local library? It's not just for books anymore! It's a goldmine of information when it comes to exploring careers. Seriously, libraries have a ton of books, magazines, and other cool stuff that can help you dive deep into all sorts of jobs and learn about different career paths. Here's how you can make your library trips super productive:

1. **Shelf Exploration:** Roam around the career and job sections in the library. You might find books about specific jobs, success stories of famous people, or even how-to guides for getting into certain industries.

2. **Magazines and Journals:** Your library probably has loads of magazines and trade journals that talk about the latest trends, cool innovations, and opportunities in various fields. These can give you a sneak peek into what it's like in the industries you're looking into.

3. **Ask the Librarian:** Librarians know their stuff, so don't be shy about asking them for help. They can point you to the right resources based on what you're interested in.

4. **Workshops and Events:** Believe it or not, some libraries host career-related events, workshops, or invite guest speakers. These can be awesome chances to learn about different jobs, meet people working in those fields, and pick up some useful career tips.

So, by taking advantage of everything your local library has to offer, you can learn a whole lot about different careers, widen your horizons, and get closer to figuring out a career path that feels right for you.

Your Network: The Power of Connections

Now, here's a super tool when it comes to checking out careers: networking. It might sound a tad intimidating, but believe me, talking to folks about their jobs can really open up opportunities for you. It can help you discover parts of the career landscape that you hadn't even noticed. Let's break down how you can amp up your networking game:

1. **Start with Your Circle:** Kick-off by talking to people you're comfortable with - friends, family, teachers, coaches, or even your neighbors. You might be surprised, they could share some interesting experiences or might know someone who can give you some real insight into a career you've been considering.

2. **Attend Events:** Keep an eye out for local happenings, workshops, or talks about subjects you're interested in. These are fantastic spots to bump into folks who are doing what you dream of doing and hear what it's actually like from them.

3. **Ask Story-Telling Questions:** When you converse with people about their careers, ask questions that encourage them to share their experiences. You'll learn more about what the job's actually like, and they'll likely find the conversation more enjoyable, too.

4. **Be Open to Meeting New People:** Each person you meet is a fresh opportunity to learn about a different career. Even a casual chat can sometimes lead to unexpected connections and job possibilities in the future.

5. **Maintain Your Connections:** After you've made a new connection, don't let it go cold! Send a thank-you message or follow them on social media. You never know when that connection might come in handy.

If you're curious to learn more about networking, be sure to head on over to the networking chapter in part 2 of the book. Scouting careers might feel like a giant quest, but with the right resources and a dash of grit, you'll start uncovering exciting prospects. Remember, through networking, you're not just learning - you're building relationships that could pave the way to your future dream job.

Exploring Non-Traditional Career Paths

As you step into this thrilling ride of career exploration, let's open the door to some out-of-the-box, up-and-coming opportunities as well. These unconventional paths could be about starting your own biz, dipping your toes into the gig economy, rocking the work-from-home life, or even landing gigs in super rad, rapidly growing areas like green energy, AI, or virtual reality. By keeping these paths on your map, you'll be ready to adapt to our fast-changing job landscape and discover a career that truly lights your fire.

So, as you flip through these pages, keep an open mind and consider how these not-so-average careers might align with your values, your passions, and your goals.

The Benefits of Non-Traditional Career Paths

Non-traditional careers come with a bunch of perks that might make them a super tempting choice for your professional journey. Here are some awesome benefits:

1. **Flexibility:** Picture this—working when you want, from wherever you fancy. A lot of non-traditional jobs let you twist work around your life, not the reverse. Less stress, more time for your favorite things—sounds like a win-win!

2. **Captain of Your Own Ship:** Many non-traditional jobs let you take the wheel. You get to decide what work you do and how you do it. It's like crafting your own career adventure, packed with stuff you're totally stoked about.

3. **Unchain Your Creativity:** Non-traditional gigs are often in super thrilling and rapidly changing fields. You'll get the chance to think outside the box, cook up fresh ideas, and push the envelope of what's possible.

4. **Heart in the Work:** Going the non-traditional route could lead to a job that really resonates with you. You get to make a real difference in something you deeply care about. And when you're passionate about what you do, it hardly feels like work, right?

5. **Learn and Grow:** Non-traditional jobs might require you to juggle many roles and tackle fresh challenges. This means you'll constantly be picking up new things and stretching your skills in a bunch of different areas.

6. **Ka-ching:** Some non-traditional jobs, especially ones where you're your own boss or have super-hot skills, can rake in some serious dough. So, if you've got big dreams of a killer gaming rig or a dream vacation, a non-traditional career might just be your fast track there.

So, as you can see, stepping off the beaten path by choosing a nontraditional career can be fun, rewarding, and a great way to make a living.

Examples of Non-Traditional Careers

We've cooked up a list of non-traditional careers, sorted into categories to ignite your imagination and nudge you to think beyond the ordinary. This list might not cover every single job out there, but it should definitely crank up your career exploration engine.

1. Technology
    - Ethical Hacker
    - Virtual Reality Designer
    - User Experience (UX) Designer
    - 3D Printing Specialist
    - Health Informatics Specialist
    - Telemedicine Practitioner
    - Augmented Reality Developer
    - Bioinformatics Scientist
    - Crypto/Blockchain Consultant
    - Algorithm Bias Auditor
    - Robotic Process Automation Developer
    - Exoskeleton Technician
    - Quantum Computing Expert
    - Cyber Security Analyst
    - Privacy Consultant
    - Data Visualization Specialist

2. Creative Industries
    - Professional Blogger/Influencer
    - Adventure Tour Guide
    - Art Therapist
    - Game Tester
    - Voice Actor
    - Food Stylist

- Escape Room Designer
- Tiny House Designer
- Virtual Event Planner

3. Environment and Sustainability
   - Urban Farmer
   - Sustainability Consultant
   - Aquaponics Farmer
   - Wellness Consultant
   - Vertical Farming Expert
   - Renewable Energy Specialist
   - Holistic Nutritionist
   - Wildfire Prevention Specialist
   - Circular Economy Specialist

4. Entrepreneurship and Business
   - Entrepreneur
   - Social Media Manager
   - Dog Trainer
   - Personal Shopper
   - Professional Organizer
   - Online Tutor/Coach
   - Genealogist
   - Life/Executive Coach
   - Animal-Assisted Therapy Practitioner

5. Unique and Emerging Fields
   - Drone Operator
   - eSports Professional
   - Space Tourism Guide
   - E-sports Coach
   - Medical Illustrator
   - Algorithm Bias Auditor

Found ones that pique your interest? Dig into these non-traditional careers, do some deep online searches, join industry forums, follow industry pros on social media, sign up for webinars or online courses. You can even listen to relevant podcasts or YouTube channels.

Remember, the job market is like a rollercoaster, always moving, always evolving, and new chances pop up every day. Use this list as a launchpad and inspiration to keep your mind open to the wide world of non-traditional careers. Don't be shy to dig deep and explore these options – you might just stumble upon a career that gets your heart racing and aligns perfectly with your passions, values, and dreams.

Staying Informed About Future Job Opportunities

With all these tech gadgets and AI robots doing tasks we used to do, the world of jobs is changing faster than you can say 'self-driving car'. But hey, don't worry - even though some jobs might fade away, brand-new ones will pop up. We're talking about jobs that might seem totally out of this world right now. Just imagine, you could be doing a job your parents could never have dreamed of!

To keep up with these cool changes, you must stay in the loop about the latest job market trends. Think of change as your ticket to growing and learning more about yourself, and make sure to keep an eye on all the hot new careers and industries. How do you do that? Stick around till the resources chapter at the end of the book!

Predicting and Preparing for Future Jobs

Let's start by looking for patterns. Which industries seem to be booming? Which tech stuff is everyone talking about? Think about topics like green energy, biotech, or even virtual reality. Where's our world headed, and how can you get ready for the ride?

The key is to stay curious and never stop learning. You want to build up a bunch of skills that you can use in different jobs, like knowing how to communicate well, solve problems, and think critically. You can do activities outside of school, like volunteering or taking online classes, to get even better at these skills. The key is to see yourself as a lifelong learner - the more flexible you are, the better you'll be at handling whatever the future throws at you.

Don't forget to explore what you love to do, too. Your passions can give you some hints about where your career might head in the future. Try making a vision board or writing in a journal about what you want your future to look like - this can help you figure out what really excites you.

Last but not least, have faith in yourself. You know what you like and what you're good at. Pair that up with what you learn about the job market, and you'll be in a great spot to guess what kind of careers could be waiting for you.

And hey, don't get stressed out about the job market changing all the time. Embrace the mystery, stay in the loop, and remember: your unique mix of skills and passions will guide you to the perfect job - even if that job doesn't exist yet.

Emerging Career Fields of the Future

Alright, let's get future-ready! We're going to explore some fields that experts reckon will be big in the future. Remember, this is a sneak peek into tomorrow, so while it's exciting, it's also just a bit of educated guessing.

1. **Green Tech and Sustainability**: Picture a world where we're all doing our part to keep Mother Earth happy. You could be right there in the thick of it, helping people learn how to live waste-free, designing bio fuels, or tackling the big one - climate change.

2. **Health Tech**: As tech gets smarter and our population gets older, there's a whole world of jobs opening up. Ever thought about becoming a doctor but doing it all online? Or helping people understand their genes? Maybe even diving into the fascinating world of biotech?

3. **Space Exploration**: Who hasn't dreamt of going to space, right? Well, the future might just have a job for you that's out of this world, literally. Imagine designing homes on Mars, guiding tourists around the moon, or finding alien life!

4. **Virtual and Augmented Reality**: Ever put on a VR headset and thought, "I could make this even cooler"? Well, here's your chance. You could be teaching in a virtual classroom, developing new AR apps, or creating immersive VR worlds.

5. **Mental Health and Wellness**: We all know how important it is to take care of our mental health, right? So why not consider a career where you get to do just that? You could be the person who helps others find balance and peace, coaches them on mindfulness, or explores new holistic ways to boost mental health.

6. **Alternative Education**: Not everyone learns the same way, and that's okay. Imagine a job where you help others find the learning style that works for them. You could be a homeschooling guru, a specialist who understands how different people learn, or even make learning fun by creating educational video games.

7. **Food Innovation**: Love food? Love science? Why not mix the two? With the need for sustainable and healthy food growing, you could be the one to create a new kind of farm, develop tasty plant-based foods, or help restaurants go zero-waste.

The world of work is a lot like a magic show, new tricks (or in this case, jobs) keep appearing. Stay curious, keep learning, and be ready to seize those new opportunities. Who knows, you might even create your own job that doesn't exist yet! How cool would that be?

In this chapter, we've navigated through various ways of pinpointing possible career paths that match your values, interests, and goals. We've checked out the things you should keep in mind when weighing up different career paths, and we've also discussed the importance of being open to both the classic and the off-the-beaten-track job options. Plus, we've discussed why it's so crucial to stay clued in about the newest industries and jobs on the scene, and why being flexible can help you roll with the changes in the job market.

As we set our sights on the next chapter, remember this: self-awareness, curiosity, and adaptability are your career compass, guiding you toward a job that's not just a paycheck, but a passion. Armed with everything you've learned so far, you're all set to plot your career course and cruise confidently toward your dream job.

Chapter 4 - What Does It Take to Achieve Your Dream?

"The only way to do great work is to love what you do." - Steve Jobs

O kay, now that you've brainstormed and have a better idea of where you want to go career-wise, you've reached a super important step: figuring out what skills you need for your dream job and how they stack up against what you've got right now.

In this chapter, we're going to crack the code on how to spot the skills, knowledge, and experience you need, to map out a plan to level up. We'll dive into everything you need to know to get where you want to go. And don't worry, we'll also help you with all the possible ways you can find this stuff out so you've got all your bases covered!

Just like a sailor uses their smarts to steer clear of stormy seas, you'll learn how to spot what you need to succeed in your career path. With this map in hand, you'll not only reach your dream job but also become the kind of person who shines in their field.

Spotting the Gaps to Your Dream Job

So, you've got this crystal-clear vision of your dream job or even a vague idea of the direction you'd like to head toward. Good stuff! But here's the fun challenge - figuring out what steps you need to take and which skills you need to master to land that dream gig.

We're here to help with that! By grasping these things, you'll be able to sketch out your path clearly and make some super-savvy decisions. Plus, if stuff gets switched up along the way (heads up: it definitely will), you'll know how to remix your plan. In this part, we're gonna explore why these things are super important and how they edge you closer to your ultimate career goal.

Getting the Right Education: Different careers have different educational requirements like degrees, certifications, or special training. Having those qualifications can give you an edge and open up amazing opportunities!

But here's the deal: the world of education is always changing. That's why it's crucial to stay informed and stay on top of what's happening in your field of interest. By doing so, you can plan your educational journey and stay one step ahead of the game.

Now, let's talk about another aspect of education - grades. They're not just numbers on a report card. They reflect your hard work, self-discipline, and commitment. Setting goals based on the grade requirements for your dream career is like aiming for the stars. It motivates you to give it your all and strive for excellence. Plus, awesome grades can lead to exciting opportunities like scholarships, grants, and incredible programs that give you a head start on your career path.

Participation in Relevant Extracurriculars: Extracurriculars are way more than just a fun-filled after-school hangout. They're your golden ticket to diving deep into what you love and scooping up some cool skills on the way.

In the world we live in today, nailing your exams isn't the be-all and end-all. There are loads of smart folks out there, and to really shine, you've gotta prove that you're about more than just acing tests. You're the type who steps up, has a passion, and is ready to dive in headfirst.

Let's use the medical field as an example. Volunteering at a local clinic or hospital isn't just a sign you're serious about your goal. It's also your pass to real-life experience that you won't find in any textbook. Or maybe you're all about tech and coding. Being on your school's robotics or coding team, or even crushing it in coding competitions, can make your college application or CV shine brighter than a supernova.

So, don't just chill on the sidelines! Dive into the stuff that gets your heart racing. Not only will you have the time of your life, but you'll also pick up some handy experience that could give you a leg up in your future career. It's all about showing future colleges or employers that you're more than a grade—you're someone who's got the passion and drive to make things happen.

Professional Network: Picture this: you know someone working at that tech company you daydream about joining. They could spill the beans about what it's like to work there and maybe even hook you up with an internship. Or imagine having a mentor who's a successful entrepreneur, guiding you through the maze of starting your own business.

There are a ton of ways to start building your network. You could check out events related to your dream career, join groups on social media that are all about your interests, or sign up with professional organizations. And you know what? We reckon networking is so key that we've whipped up an entire chapter about it! So stick around, because we've got heaps more to share on this.

Practical Experience: You know how you can read all about soccer from a book, but won't really get the hang of it until you've kicked a ball around on the field? That's the gist of getting practical experience. It's all about taking what you've absorbed in the classroom (or on your own) and giving it a whirl in the real world.

Internships, volunteering, co-op programs, or even part-time gigs can serve up a slice of what your dream job is really like. And hey, this isn't just about scoring awesome experiences to jazz up your resume (though that's a killer perk!). It's also about test-driving things and figuring out if it's genuinely what you want to do.

Let's say you've got your heart set on being a vet because you're all about animals. But then, you land an internship at a vet clinic and realize it's not exactly the furry cuddle-fest you'd imagined. Well, wouldn't it be nifty to know that before you've committed years to vet school?

Remember, each experience, even if it's not exactly what you thought, is a step towards fine-tuning your path and setting you apart from the pack.

Personal Brand and Online Presence: Your online presence is the narrative you spin about yourself for the entire world, and trust me, folks are tuning in (and definitely Googling!).

Your personal brand is your spotlight moment to show off what makes you, unmistakably you. It's your platform to celebrate all the stuff you've accomplished, the skills you've scored, and the values you stand for. It's your chance to dazzle with your unique brand of cool.

With so much of our daily lives shifting online, it's mega important to keep a professional persona on the web. This could be via social media channels like LinkedIn or even your own personal website. Think of it as a round-the-clock, always fresh, virtual resume ready to wow on demand.

Let's say you're itching to break into game design. Picture owning a website where you flaunt the games you've crafted, blog about your takes on the industry, and share your sources of inspiration. Or perhaps you're a budding journalist, so you kick-start a blog where you report on local buzz. You'll be amazed at how many opportunities can swing your way once you start airing your passions online.

Soft Skills: Nope, I'm not talking about perfecting your soft serve ice cream swirl (though, let's admit, that's a pretty fun skill). I'm referring to gems like communication, teamwork, problem-solving, and adaptability.

Let's decode these a bit. Communication is all about expressing yourself like a pro. Are you clear and considerate when you chat or pen down your thoughts? Can you break down your ideas so that others get your drift? Teamwork? That's all about gelling with your crew. Can you brainstorm, share visions, and rally your team toward victory? Problem-solving is about thinking on your toes and conjuring solutions to obstacles. And adaptability? That's all about bobbing and weaving as circumstances shift.

These super skills are important because they turn you into a stellar teammate, an innovative thinker, and a reliable go-getter. They're the skills that make you, unmistakably, you! And the best part? They're handy in any career you pick.

Certification or Licensing: Imagine you've finally scored your dream gig as a professional counselor. You're geared up to start, but there's a slight hiccup. You require a license to kick-start your practice in your state. Whoops!

That's precisely why it's crucial to be in the know if your chosen career demands any special certifications or licenses. Imagine them as a driver's license but for your career. I mean, you wouldn't just hop in a car and zoom off without a license, right? The same principle applies to certain professions.

So if your dream job requires a certification or license, start crafting a strategy to achieve it. Sure, it might be a bit of added work, but when you're busy doing a job that sets your heart on fire, it'll feel like a cakewalk. Plus, it's an awesome way to showcase to future employers that you've got the goods to ace the job.

Language Skills: If your dream job involves you globe-trotting or collaborating with people from diverse nations. Or, if you've got your heart set on living and working in a foreign country you may need to be fluent in more languages than just English.

Language know-how can be uber important for gigs that have you working with international folks. Imagine being a diplomat who's lost in translation in the country you're assigned to. Or a global sales wiz who can't connect with clients in their mother tongue. Yikes, talk about a hurdle!

There are tons of ways to polish your language skills or even pick up a new language from scratch. Consider taking language classes at school or maybe online. Ever heard of language immersion programs? You actually live in a foreign country and learn the lingo by using it daily.

So, if your dream job has an international vibe, see if you'll need to be proficient in another language. If the answer's yes, then get started already. It won't just make your job smoother, but it's also a great skill to have up your sleeve. Bonus - being bilingual or multilingual can make you stand out amidst a sea of job seekers!

I know this might feel like a ton to digest, but hold on! Tackle these points one by one, and you'll soon become a whiz at figuring out the ins and outs of landing your dream job. It's all about making sharp decisions and setting achievable goals.

Now that we've skimmed over all the skills and requirements for your career that you need to mull over, let's talk about where to hunt for all the inside scoop on your future career. Trust me, there's a plethora of resources just waiting to be tapped into, all set to help you lock your sights on your dream job.

Uncovering the Requirements: Key Resources and Strategies

Consider this section to be your ultimate guidebook, full of amazing resources and smart strategies that'll help you uncover all the gaps to get you to the career you're aiming for. With this guidebook in your backpack, you'll be all set to plot your path, make awesome choices, and eventually reach your career goals.

Research Job Listings

Online job listings are goldmines—they're bursting with clues about what it takes to land your dream job. These listings don't just tell you about the job, but they also spill the beans on what employers want in their dream candidate. Degrees, certifications or certifications? Years of experience? Particular work they want you to have done? It's all there, spelled out for you.

And that's not all! Some job posts also shout out language requirements—especially important if you fancy working in a multinational company or a workplace that loves diversity. They'll also throw in a list of soft skills they want you to master.

So dive into those job listings and discover what you need to get a head start on your dream career.

Conduct Informational Interviews

When you take a dive into informational interviews, you get to unearth some top-tier knowledge and inside info that's tough to dig up anywhere else. Plus, you learn about the kind of real-world experience you need, which can help you morph into the perfect fit for the job.

Informational interviews can also open up killer networking opportunities, which are essential in today's job market. And the cherry on top? You get tips on how to brand yourself and suggestions for after-school stuff that can amp up your resume.

So, how about giving it a shot? Reach out to professionals in the field you're eyeing and ask if they'd be down for an informational interview. Who knows? This could be the secret code to cracking open your dream career! And don't worry, we'll be diving deeper into the world of informational interviewing in the networking chapter in part 2 of this book, so you know exactly what to ask them.

Career-focused Websites

On the journey to your dream career, websites specifically catered towards career development become your trusted companions. Rich with insights, these sites help sketch out the educational route to your desired destination, suggesting the perfect blend of extracurricular engagements and hands-on experience that could make your profile gleam.

Keeping pace with the constantly evolving industry trends is crucial, and these websites serve as your reliable update hubs. They also extend their utility as networking guides, illustrating how to build and foster professional connections that could shape your career trajectory significantly.

And when it comes to crafting a compelling digital persona, these sites provide invaluable advice on establishing and maintaining a striking online presence. We've listed a couple to get you started in the resources chapter at the end of the book. So, invest some time exploring these sites, and you'll find yourself equipped with the knowledge to confidently stride towards your career aspirations.

School Counselors

We've mentioned school counselors and teachers before and we'll mention them again because they really are invaluable allies on your journey towards your destination career. They're well-versed in the educational qualifications and grade requirements you'll need to meet and can provide guidance on which courses to take and how to excel in them. They can also recommend extracurricular activities that'll boost your resume and help you gain valuable experience. Plus, they're often great resources for developing soft skills, which are crucial to succeeding in any career.

And don't be surprised if they even have connections to industry professionals who can offer additional advice and insights. Last but not least, they can guide you on any necessary certification or licensing requirements specific to your field.

Diving into Professional Associations, Industry Groups, and Online Communities

Alright, here's a winning move - get involved in groups or clubs that are all about your field of interest. Imagine it, mingling (even if it's online) with folks who are already living your dream job. They're a goldmine of stories, tips, and advice. They can even let you in on specifics about certain certificates or licenses you might need down the road.

These groups often throw events like workshops, meetups, or even conferences where you can learn a ton and connect with more people (sometimes for zero cost!). And let's not forget about the insider info on things like job openings or the latest trends in the field. Being part of these groups is like having a VIP pass to your dream career.

You'll also find a support system in peers who are on the same path as you. So jump into online communities and forums – they're your secret weapon in reaching your career goals! To kick off, check out some of the online communities linked in the resources section.

And there you have it! Tap into these resources and professionals and you'll get a clear picture of what it takes to achieve your career goals.

As we seal this chapter, remember that this trek isn't about simply crossing items off a to-do list. It's about grasping the full spectrum of what your chosen journey involves and recognizing the zones where you need to level up. It's about viewing the complete panorama and understanding how you slot into it.

You're not meant to have all the answers just yet. Instead of feeling disheartened by these gaps, let's greet them as the next thrilling level on our quest.

In our next chapter, we'll switch gears from identification to action mode. We'll equip you with strategies to buff up the skills you need, leverage your strengths, and assemble a toolkit that will help you bridge the gap between your current position and your end goal. So, let's plunge into the realm of skill development and start transforming your career dreams into your reality!

Chapter 5 - Bridging the Gap & Leveling Up

"Education is the passport to the future, for tomorrow belongs to those who prepare for it today." - Malcolm X

We've journeyed together through the twists and turns of figuring out who you are and what career you're interested in. And now you've probably noticed some gaps between where you're at now and where you want to be. But remember, these gaps aren't roadblocks, they're actually stepping stones for you to learn and grow.

Our mission now is to close up these gaps by working on and sharpening the skills and knowledge you'll need for your future job path. We're going to explore practical ways to beef up your abilities, from getting tech-savvy to nailing those soft skills, getting a grip on your time, and maybe even going for more schooling or training.

Let's kick off this journey of skill-building by first planting the seed of a mindset that's super important for any career these days - the power of never-ending learning.

Harnessing the Power of Continuous Learning

In a world that's always on the move, the real champs are the ones who know that learning never ends. With new tech popping up all the time, society shifting, and the economy doing its thing, learning for life is more than just a cool idea—it's a must-have.

Staying in the know about what's trending in your industry is super important. This could be as easy as reading some articles about your field, catching a webinar or conference, or chatting in online forums. It's about making learning a part of your day-to-day, as normal as grabbing a bite to eat or getting sleep.

But beyond just being a part of your routine, non-stop learning is a way of thinking. It's about growing what psychologist Carol Dweck calls a "growth mindset" (remember chapter 1?)—the idea that with some time, effort, and grit, you can get better and smarter. This way of thinking keeps you pushing forward, taking on challenges, and seeing hard work as the way to become a master at what you do.

Bottom line, continuous learning isn't just about picking up new knowledge or skills; it's about rolling with change, staying curious, and always aiming to be the best you can be. It's about realizing that the journey of learning is basically the journey of life. Embrace it, and you'll be ready to rock in the future job market.

Building Your Technical Skills Toolbox

In today's job market, technical skills are a huge deal. As technology keeps changing and sneaking into every kind of job out there, employers are seeking candidates who have a whole bunch of different tech skills. These skills not only open the doors to a whole lot of different job possibilities, but they also make you stand out in the field you've chosen. Whether it's being a whiz at a certain software, knowing how to code, or being a pro at analyzing data, tech skills are the tools you'll use to build your successful future.

So, you're probably wondering how you can start collecting these super important tech skills? There are many paths you can take.

School classes are one of the easiest ways to go. A lot of schools have classes in things like computer science, digital design, and engineering, which give you a good base to build on. Be on the lookout for classes that line up with what you're interested in as a career and can help you pick up the tech skills you'll need.

Workshops and training programs, both in-person and online, are also really great resources. These usually focus on specific skills and give you a chance to get your hands dirty, which helps you understand and apply what you're learning even better.

Internships or work experience programs are another awesome way to pick up tech skills. You not only get to try your hand at the real thing, but you also get a sneak peek at what a professional work environment is like, giving you a real-life look at what your future career might be like.

Online learning platforms, like Coursera, Udemy, or Khan Academy have courses in all sorts of fields, letting you learn at your own speed and usually giving you a certificate when you finish.

Speaking of certificates, it's worth mentioning that having certificates that are recognized by the industry can really pump up your professional profile. Certificates are solid proof of your tech know-how and your dedication to your field, making you really stand out to potential employers. Whether it's a certificate in project management, a coding language, or a specific software, these credentials are golden on your resume.

Tech skills aren't just something to check off your career to-do list; they're cornerstone pieces that can shape your professional journey. So, dive in, explore, and start stocking up your tech skills garage today. Remember, every skill you pick up brings you one step closer to the career you want.

Soft Skills: The Unseen Powerhouse of Professional Success

Sure, technical skills are pretty key, but they're not the whole deal. Your soft skills are just as, if not more, important. These are things like communication, teamwork, problem-solving, and emotional smarts. They're like your secret weapon for rocking your career, even though they don't always get the spotlight they deserve.

So, what are soft skills anyway? Unlike hard skills, which are specific things you can learn, soft skills are a bit trickier to pin down. They're about how you connect with others, how you handle work, and how you cope under different circumstances. It's not just about knowing the right fork to use at a business lunch or being able to work in a team – it's about human connections, being flexible, and understanding emotions.

Let's break it down with an example: Imagine a project manager who knows all the technical stuff to get a project done, but can't clearly communicate the project's vision, or inspire their team. That project might hit a wall. But a project manager who might not be a tech wizard but is a pro at motivating their team, handling conflicts, and building consensus, is probably going to nail that project.

Let's dive into some soft skills that you should totally focus on, no matter what career you're dreaming of:

Communication: Boost this skill by practicing active listening, writing clearly and simply, and trying out public speaking or debating.

Teamwork: Join team sports, group projects, or volunteer gigs that need collaboration and cooperation.

Adaptability: Try new things, like traveling, picking up a new hobby, or tackling unfamiliar tasks in your part-time job. Every new experience helps you grow this skill.

Problem-Solving: Challenge yourself with puzzles, strategic games, or leadership roles that need you to come up with creative solutions.

Emotional Intelligence: Practice mindfulness and empathy, ask for feedback, and think about how you react to different situations.

Getting involved in extracurricular activities, volunteering, or joining clubs and organizations are also awesome ways to work on your soft skills. You'll often have to work as part of a team, solve problems, take the lead, and communicate effectively, all of which help build your soft skills.

Working on your soft skills has tons of long-term benefits. You'll probably enjoy your job more because you'll be better at dealing with the ups and downs of the workplace. You'll be able to build stronger relationships, both at work and in your personal life, because you'll understand your own and other people's emotions better. Plus, you'll be more adaptable, which is essential in a job market that's always changing.

In short, soft skills are like your secret superpower for a successful career. By spending time working on these skills, you're setting yourself up for a really rewarding career.

Exploring Education and Training Options after High School

As high school becomes a speck in your rear-view mirror and you rev up for the big, wide world, you'll come across a ton of routes for further education and training. Each path has its own way to boost your skills, expand your job prospects, and set you on the highway to a killer career. In this section, we'll take a pit stop at each of these routes: vocational schools, community colleges, apprenticeships, online learning platforms, and good old traditional four-year colleges and universities.

Vocational Schools

These schools are all about getting you ready for specific jobs that you're passionate about with specialized training that can give you a head start in your career.

One of the great things about vocational schools is that you can finish them much quicker than traditional four-year colleges. This means you can dive into the working world sooner and start earning money doing what you love. It's like taking the express lane to your dream career!

Another advantage of vocational schools is that they focus on practical, hands-on training. You won't just be sitting in classrooms, but you'll be getting your hands dirty and gaining real-world experience. This can make you feel more confident and prepared when you step into the professional world.

However, it's important to consider a few things before committing to a vocational school. While these schools provide specialized training, they might not offer as many detours if you decide to change your career or explore different subjects later on. So, it's essential to have a clear idea of the career path you want to pursue before enrolling in a vocational school.

But don't worry! Vocational schools offer a wide range of career paths to choose from. Whether you're interested in becoming a skilled tradesperson, a healthcare professional, a culinary artist, or a graphic designer, there's a vocational program out there for you. These schools often collaborate with industry professionals and provide hands-on internships, giving you valuable connections and real-world experience.

To get a better idea of what's available, check out your local vocational schools and explore their programs. Talk to graduates, industry professionals, and even attend open houses or virtual tours to get a feel for the environment. It's all about finding the right fit for your passions and goals.

So, if you're ready to jump into a specific career path and fast-track your way to success, vocational schools can be an exciting option to consider.

Community Colleges

Community Colleges are like pit stops on your journey to success, offering a chance to earn a two-year associate degree or certifications in lots of different areas. And guess what? They won't break the bank like some four-year colleges! That means you can get a great education without emptying your wallet.

Community colleges also often have agreements with four-year universities, so you can transfer your credits and keep going to earn a bachelor's degree if you want. It's like a smooth transition to a higher level of education without the hefty price tag. How cool is that?

One of the things that make community colleges special is their smaller class sizes. Forget those giant lecture halls! At a community college, you'll experience a more personal and cozy learning environment. You can really get to know your professors and classmates, ask questions, and get extra support when you need it. It's like being part of a close-knit community where everyone is there to help you succeed.

When it comes to programs and areas of study, community colleges have a wide variety to choose from. Whether you're interested in business, computers, healthcare, arts, or trades, there's something for everyone. These colleges offer practical, career-focused programs that give you the skills and hands-on training you need for the real world.

To get started, you can research community colleges in your area and check out what they have to offer. Take virtual tours, attend information sessions, or even chat with current students to get a feel for the campus vibes. And don't forget to reach out to advisors who can guide you through the enrollment process and help you make smart choices about your education.

So, if you're looking for an affordable and flexible educational path, community colleges are an awesome choice.

Apprenticeships

In an apprenticeship, you learn by doing – on the job and in the classroom, and you get paid while you're at it! You can find apprenticeships in a range of industries, like construction, manufacturing, and IT. It's a hands-on way to gain valuable skills and experience while earning some cash.

Here's how it works: You'll work alongside experienced professionals who will teach you the ins and outs of the trade. You'll get to apply what you learn right away, getting real-world experience that can't be matched. But it's not just about working. You'll also spend time in the classroom, where you'll learn the technical knowledge and theory that goes hand in hand with your practical skills.

Keep in mind that apprenticeships can be quite competitive. There are only a limited number of spots available, so you'll need to bring your A-game and show your passion and dedication. It may take some time and effort to find the right apprenticeship for you, but trust me, it's worth it!

Apprenticeships can also require a significant commitment. You'll be working and learning at the same time, which means you'll have to manage your time wisely. It can be challenging, but it's also incredibly rewarding. Not only will you be gaining valuable skills and knowledge, but you'll also be earning a paycheck while you do it. Talk about a win-win situation!

So, if you're someone who loves getting their hands dirty, enjoys being in a real work environment, and wants to kick-start their career with practical skills, apprenticeships are a fantastic option.

Online Learning Platforms

With awesome sites like Coursera, edX, and Udacity, you can take courses from top-tier universities and learn from industry gurus. It's like having a buffet of subjects right at your fingertips!

One of the coolest things about online learning is the flexibility it offers. You can learn at your own pace, whenever and wherever you want. Whether you're a night owl or an early bird, you can fit your studies into your schedule. Plus, you can choose from a wide range of subjects, from computer science to art history, and everything in between. The options are endless!

Keep in mind that online learning is a bit different from the traditional classroom experience. It requires self-discipline and motivation to stay on track. You'll need to be responsible for managing your time and staying focused on your studies. It's like having a personal learning adventure, where you set the pace and navigate your own educational journey.

So, if you're someone who loves the freedom to learn at your own pace and explore a variety of subjects, online learning platforms are perfect for you.

Four-Year Colleges and Universities

When you enroll in a four-year college or university, you're not just getting an education. You're joining a community filled with resources, support, and opportunities. From state-of-the-art libraries to cutting-edge research labs, these institutions have it all. And let's not forget about the clubs, sports teams, and other extracurricular activities that make college life so exciting.

One of the great things about four-year colleges and universities is the variety of courses available. You can explore different subjects, discover new passions, and even change your major if you want to. It's like having a buffet of knowledge right at your fingertips!

But here's the deal, tuition, housing, and other expenses can add up quickly. So, it's important to consider your financial situation and explore scholarships, grants, and financial aid options to make it more affordable.

While four-year colleges and universities offer a wealth of opportunities, they're not for everyone. If you're someone who loves the idea of a vibrant campus life, networking with professors and classmates, and immersing yourself in a wide range of courses, they might be the perfect fit for you.

Remember, the choice of education and training after high school is a personal one. Consider your interests, goals, and financial situation when deciding which path to take. And don't forget, there's no right or wrong choice. What matters most is finding an educational journey that aligns with your dreams and aspirations.

Whether you choose vocational schools, community colleges, apprentice-ships, online learning platforms, or four-year colleges and universities, each path has its own unique advantages and considerations. Take the time to explore these options, consider your interests and goals, and make an informed decision that suits you best. When you're scoping out these routes, it's crucial to think about how much they'll cost and what financial aid you could get.

The secret to making a killer decision is doing heaps of research and thinking about what truly rings your bell. Take your time to weigh the pros and cons of each option. To help you out with your research, we've linked some resources at the end of the book to help you with your research.

Exploring Gap Years: An Alternative Route to Career Discovery

What's a Gap Year, You Ask? Alright, let's get the ball rolling by understanding what a gap year is all about. It's pretty straightforward. A gap year is like a timeout, a year-long break some students opt for between high school and college, or sometimes between college years. But why on earth would they do that? There are loads of reasons! Some might need a chill break after high school, others have a serious travel bug to cure, and some want to get their hands dirty with some real-world work experience.

Going for a gap year can pack some awesome perks. For starters, you get to learn new stuff, meet all sorts of people, and see the world through a fresh pair of eyes. It's also your ticket to getting some real-world work chops, which can be super useful when you're trying to piece together what you want to do with your life. Plus, it's a golden opportunity to dip your toes in different interests and passions, which can guide you to pick a major or career path.

So, how do you ensure your gap year isn't just a long vacation but a productive adventure? Begin by drawing out some goals. What's your endgame for the gap year? Next, chalk out your activities. These could be things like traveling, volunteering, scoring internships, or even starting your own business. Ensure these activities sync with your goals and will help you level up both personally and professionally.

Like everything else, gap years do come with some potential bumps. You might worry about lagging behind your pals or losing your academic momentum. But hey, don't sweat it, you can keep your grey cells active by hopping onto online courses or reading up on stuff that gets you excited. And remember, everyone's journey is unique, so don't get caught in the comparison trap.

There's a massive buffet of amazing opportunities for your gap year. There are programs that mix travel with learning, chances to volunteer locally or overseas, internships that can offer a sneak peek into a potential career, or you could even kick off your own venture! The world is your playground, and your gap year is your green light to explore it.

In the grand scheme of things, remember, a gap year is just that – a single year. It's a moment in the timeline of your life. But if played right, it can be a powerful instrument for self-discovery and career exploration. So, if you're feeling the thrill of adventure and fancy stepping off the usual route, a gap year might be just the ticket!

The Power of a Diverse Skill Set

Picture your career journey as a bustling ocean of opportunities, ever-changing and full of surprises. Now, imagine your skill set as a sturdy, well-stocked toolbox - one that equips you to be flexible, resilient, and ready to face a vast range of career challenges. This flexibility broadens your horizons, enhancing your employability, and offering you a wider selection of career paths.

Cultivating transferable skills is a crucial step in amassing a diverse skill set. These are skills that hold their value across varied areas and industries. Skills like problem-solving, leadership, communication, and project management – are the real game-changers, regardless of whether you're a software whiz, a creative graphic designer, a meticulous project manager, or a dedicated teacher.

However, don't get the wrong idea. Specialization definitely has its place. It's what sets you apart, making you a sought-after expert in your field. The trick is to strike the right balance between being a generalist and a specialist. As they say, "Being a jack of all trades doesn't mean you must be a master of none." Strive to find balance.

So, how do you go about assembling this mixed bag of skills? Begin by recognizing your interests and acknowledging the skills you already possess. Then, think about what other skills could work well with these. Let's say you're a coding pro but public speaking sends chills down your spine. Maybe joining a debate club or signing up for a communication class could be your next move to level up your presentation skills.

Always remember that learning is an endless journey. By keeping up with the learning curve and diversifying your skills, you'll be all set to adapt to changes and grab hold of new opportunities as they come along. So, stay intrigued, keep the learning flame alive, and harness the magic of a diverse skill set.

As we sail into the next chapter, we'll assist you in transforming all this insightful information into a practical, implementable blueprint for your future. Are you pumped to sketch the plan? Let's embark on the next leg of our journey, together.

This chapter has taken you on a wild ride through skill development, highlighting the big deal of technical skills and soft skills. We've looked at a ton of options for learning and training after high school to fill the gaps. We've also stressed the importance of being adaptable, continuously learning, and developing a wide range of skills.

As we keep moving, remember that these skills and pieces of knowledge are the tools you need to build your future. They're the foundation that you'll build your career on.

Alright, up next, we'll dive into a fun blueprint-making session in the next chapter to fill those gaps and get you on the fast track to your dream job!

Chapter 6 - Making The Plan

"A goal without a plan is just a wish." - Antoine de Saint-Exupéry

It's game time! It's about time we take all these puzzle pieces and whip up your blueprint for the future. You've put in the effort to get to know yourself better, to really vibe with your values, interests, and what makes you, well, you. No matter where you are in your life journey – still navigating high school, cruising through college, or elsewhere – you've delved into the world of career possibilities, whittled down your options, and figured out what you'll need to hit your targets. So, what comes next? Here comes the fun part. It's time to craft your master plan!

A plan is like a trusty compass that keeps you on track as you navigate the winding path to your career dreams. It's your secret map, helping you find your way through the dense forest of personal growth, skill-building, and reaching for the stars. A solid plan is like a well-packed backpack, well-organized, realistic, and ready to roll with the punches, considering life's habit of throwing curve balls at us.

But how do you go about creating this epic plan? Kick-off by slicing your goals into smaller, bite-sized tasks. Work out what steps you need to take to knock out each task and set up deadlines to keep yourself on track. Keep in mind, your plan needs to be flexible enough to bob and weave around unexpected obstacles but structured enough to keep you marching in the right direction.

In this chapter, we're going to take a deep dive into creating a plan that's tailor-made for you, turning your dreams from mere fantasy into absolute reality. Remember, everyone's path to success is as unique as their fingerprint. So, let's team up and create a plan that fits your needs, goals, and ambitions like a glove. Let's turn those dreams into reality!

What Kind of Plan Are We Going to Make? A Smart One!

Stoked to dive into planning? Let's get to it! We're going to whip up a SMART plan. Hold up, what's a SMART plan? SMART stands for Specific, Measurable, Achievable, Relevant, and Time-Bound. Let's slice these up and check them out in action.

Specific: You gotta get all the details down. Figure out exactly what steps you have to take and what goals you want to crush. By cutting your huge goals into smaller, specific tasks, you can handle them way more easily.

Right: "I will finish my homework and apply to five graphic design programs at local colleges before December 1st."

Wrong: "I will apply to a few art schools."

In the right example, the goal is crystal clear. It says exactly what needs to be done: researching and applying to five graphic design programs. It even has a due date: before December 1st. The wrong example, though, is pretty blurry. It doesn't tell us how many applications, what type of programs, or when it needs to be done. It leaves a lot of room for guesswork and might lead to procrastinating or not putting in enough effort.

Measurable: How do you know you're making headway? By setting clear checkpoints or numbers to check off your progress! Make every task or goal in your plan countable. Basically, try and figure out what you'll count, like the number of job applications you send out or the hours you clock in volunteering. Always make sure you can put a number to your plan and your progress.

Right: "I'm going to clock in 20 hours of volunteer work at the local community center before summer wraps up."

Wrong: "I'll do a bit of volunteer work."

The right example is a winner because it gives us a clear number to aim for, 20 hours of volunteer work. Plus, it sets a deadline: before summer is over. This makes it easy to track progress and know when the goal is smashed. The wrong example, however, is vague. How much is "a bit" of volunteer work? Without a specific number or timeframe, it's hard to measure progress or know when the goal is achieved. That's why it's so crucial to make your plans measurable!

Achievable: Your plan should aim high, but you've also gotta keep it within reach. Think about what skills you have right now, what resources are at your disposal, and what obstacles you might face. Then, mold your plan to fit. It's all about finding the sweet spot between pushing yourself and setting goals you can realistically reach. This balance is key to keeping your motivation revved up.

Right: "I'm going to level up my public speaking skills by joining a local Toastmasters club and nailing five speeches over the next half-year."

Wrong: "I'll turn into a Steve Jobs level epic public speaker in a month."

Why is the right example hitting the mark? Well, it sets a challenging but achievable goal: delivering five speeches at a Toastmasters club over six months. It also has a clear plan on how to get there: by joining a Toastmasters club. The wrong example, though, is shooting way too high. Having Steve Jobs' level of public speaking is an awesome goal, but doing it in a month is probably not going to happen. This kind of lofty goal can lead to frustration and feeling burned out. So remember, keep your goals challenging but achievable!

Relevant: Each step in your plan should align with what you want to score in your career. This means checking up on your plan often to make sure every task or goal is actually pushing you closer to your endgame.

Right: "I'm going to attend networking events focused on the healthcare industry so I can talk to professionals in the field and hear about job openings."

Wrong: "I'm going to go to random networking events to meet people."

Why's the right example on target? It's because it lays out a clear and relevant strategy: attending healthcare-specific networking events to learn about job openings and meet pros in the field. This approach directly supports a career goal in healthcare. The wrong example, however, is vague and might not be super relevant. Going to random networking events might not help if those events aren't related to your career interests. You could end up spending heaps of time without making the right connections. So remember, keep your tasks and goals relevant!

Time-bound: Deadlines are a big deal when it comes to making a plan. By setting specific time frames for each task or goal, you light a fire under your own seat. This helps you stay on track and keeps your momentum rolling.

Right: "I'm going to wrap up an online marketing course within the next three months."

Wrong: "I'm going to finish an online marketing course... someday."

Why's the right example the way to go? Because it sets a clear and specific deadline: finish an online marketing course in three months. This goal lights a fire under you, which can help keep you motivated and on task. On the other hand, the wrong example is as vague as it gets. Saying you'll do something "someday" doesn't provide any urgency or specific timeline, making it easy to procrastinate or forget about the task altogether. So, when you're setting your goals, make sure they're time-bound!

Here's what a SMART plan looks like for a high school student dreaming of a career in graphic design:

Specific: Research graphic design programs at nearby colleges, join the school's art club, and create a killer online portfolio of personal design projects.

Measurable: Apply to at least five graphic design programs, attend art club meetings every week, and add two new projects to the online portfolio each month.

Achievable: Assess current artistic skills and figure out if additional art courses or workshops are needed for improvement; consider time and money limits when picking graphic design programs.

Relevant: Each step in the plan should contribute to the overall goal of launching a graphic design career, from sharpening skills and building a portfolio to snagging a spot in an education program.

Time-bound: Set deadlines for finishing each step, like submitting college applications by December 1st, joining the art club within the first month of school, and updating the online portfolio monthly.

By using the SMART system in your career planning process, you're setting yourself up for a solid, effective plan that will guide you through the exciting journey toward your career goals.

Chasing your ultimate career goal might feel like you're at the bottom of a ginormous mountain right now. So, let's make the climb a bit less daunting! By creating milestones, or mini-goals, you create a path of stepping stones leading straight up to your big, beautiful goal. Let's explore how to break down your massive goals into bite-sized chunks and make them shine.

Breaking Down Big Goals Into Smaller Ones

Feeling a little swamped? Don't sweat it! You're already steps ahead of many folks your age! We're here to guide you through crafting your SMART plan.

First up, we're going to take that big, daunting career goal of yours and slice it up into more manageable mini-goals. These are going to be your milestones - the markers that show you're on the right track toward your ultimate aim. So, here's how you do it...

Identify your ultimate career goal: Start by pinpointing your long-term career goal. This is the ultimate destination you're working towards and should reflect your passions, values, and interests. This is the grand prize you're hustling for, and it should be something that sets your heart on fire and aligns with what you care about most. Having a crystal-clear picture of this goal is super important because it's going to be the fuel that keeps your engine running.

For instance, let's say your dream is to make it big as an architect. Your long-haul goal might be to land a gig at a swanky architecture firm, or maybe you've got your sights set on launching your own practice someday.

Break it down into stages: Once you've identified your ultimate career goal, divide it into several stages that represent significant steps in your journey. Think of these phases like episodes in your own career TV show, where each one builds on the one before and moves you closer to your big finale.

For example, you might break it down like this:

- High School: Excel in relevant subjects, join the school's design club, and flex your skills in architecture-related contests.
- College: Pursue a degree in architecture, get your feet wet with internships, and join clubs that are all about your field.
- Early Career: Gain experience by working in a renowned architecture firm, show up at industry events, and weave a solid professional network.

Mark Your Milestones for Each Phase: Inside each phase, spot the key milestones that'll push you toward your big career dream. These milestones are smaller, doable steps that will act like pit stops on your journey.

For instance, let's look at the high school phase of your architect dream. You could mark these milestones:

- Score an A or better in your math and art classes to lay a solid groundwork for your future studies.
- Sign up for the school's design club and really get into the club's activities and projects.
- Jump into at least one architecture-related contest each year to get your hands dirty and show off your skills.

By pinpointing your big career dream, slicing it into phases, and marking milestones in each phase, you'll sketch out a clear road map that'll steer you toward your dream career. This way, you'll keep your eyes on the prize, stay pumped up, and hold on to your grit as you work to hit each milestone and, in the end, your big career dream.

Now Let's Make Those Milestones and Timelines SMART!

You've got your timeline and milestones all set up. Nice! Now, let's double-check to make sure each of those milestones is as SMART as it can be.

SMART-ing up your milestones is a big deal. It's like drawing a detailed map for your journey, helping you stay on the right path and make any tweaks needed as you go along. We're mentioning it again so that it sticks! This really does make a difference!

Here's how to make your milestones SMART:

Specific: Get detailed about what each milestone is. Ditch the vague stuff. Instead of "Get better grades," go for "Boost my math grade to an A by the end of the semester."

Measurable: Slap a number on each milestone. This way, you can keep track of how you're doing. So, instead of "Join a club," try "Sign up for two clubs related to my career dreams by the end of the school year."

Achievable: Give each milestone a reality check. You want them to be challenging but doable. So, instead of "Become a French-speaking pro in a month," write "Finish an online French course by summer's end."

Relevant: Make sure each milestone lines up with your career dreams. If you're aiming to be a software engineer, a relevant milestone could be "Finish an intro to programming course in Python."

Time-bound: Slap a due date on each milestone. This helps you keep the pedal to the metal. So, instead of "Apply to internships," try "Send out applications to at least five internships by December 1st."

If you're a visual learner, making your plan visual (using a flowchart or diagram) can really help. We've illustrated a sample career plan visual in the resources section. Be sure to check it out!

Keep in mind that this is just an example and you should most definitely adapt it to fit your individual circumstances (even if you're aiming to be a graphic design superstar!). Remember it's never too late or early to start. Take it one (SMART) step at a time and you will reach your goal!

Tips to Help You Stick to Your Plan

Want to crush those career goals? Well, sticking to your plan is the secret sauce. Here are a bunch of tips to help you stay glued to your game plan:

Regular Check-ins: Make it a habit to catch up with your milestones and see how far you've journeyed. This keeps the endgame in sight and lets you adjust your strategy on the go.

Don't Forget to Set Reminders: Use calendar apps, to-do lists, or any tool that keeps you on top of important dates and tasks. It's all about keeping that momentum going.

Organize Your Life: Keep all your career planning goodies - notes, docs, resources - all in one place. So, when you need something, it's right there waiting for you. Plus, it keeps everything neat and tidy.

Find Your Cheerleaders: Get some trusted pals, family, or mentors in on your plan. They can offer advice, be your personal cheer squad, and hold you accountable, which can be super helpful.

Celebrate the Little Things: Every milestone you reach, no matter how tiny, is a big win. So, don't forget to throw a mini party! It can give your motivation a turbo boost and remind you why you're on this journey.

Stay in the Know: Keep learning about your career path and related fields. This helps you make savvy decisions and keeps you clued in on the latest trends and opportunities.

Visualize Your Victory: Picture yourself nailing those goals and how epic that's gonna feel. This can help keep you pumped and ready to stick to your plan.

Balance is Key: Chasing your dreams doesn't mean going all in, all the time. Make sure to chill out, enjoy your favorite hobbies, and recharge. Remember, you're not just planning a career, but a life too. It's not a sprint, it's a marathon. Take care of your mind and body. Good sleep, nutritious food, exercise, and chill time are not indulgences; they're essentials!

Be Like Water: If your situation or goals take a detour, be ready to adjust your plan. Career planning is a journey, so stay flexible and keep your eyes peeled for shiny new opportunities.

Always remember, sticking to your plan is a journey, not a one-time thing, and perseverance is your best friend on the road to success.

Finding the Right Balance: Sticking to Your Plan vs. Changing It

You see, as you hustle to reach your dream job, you'll be dancing on a tightrope between following your plan to the letter and knowing when to shake things up. Plans are fantastic for keeping you on track, but hey, life's a wild ride and sometimes you gotta roll with the punches. So here's a couple of pointers on how to keep things balanced:

Plans are your best buds, not your bosses: Your plan is there to back you up, not boss you around. Be cool with shaking things up when you've got to. Think of your plan as a buddy who's always changing and growing, just like you.

Take a moment to ponder: If you're thinking of switching up your plan, really give it a thought. Is it because something's different, or are you just getting cold feet or feeling pooped? Figuring out why you want to change can help you decide if it's a smart move.

Learn to spot the difference between a minor hiccup and a major hiccup. We all trip up now and then, but that doesn't always mean you need to change your plan. Sometimes, they're just teeny-weeny speed bumps that you can zoom over with a bit more elbow grease. But if you smack into a wall, well, it might be time for a rethink.

Before you switch up your plan, think about the consequences and aftereffects. Will this change get you closer to your dream job, or will it put you on the slow track? Be honest with yourself about what your decision could mean.

Being flexible is a superpower, but don't lose your bullseye (the one you see yourself hitting after all those milestones). Even if you tweak your plan, make sure it still points to your dream job.

If you're on the fence about whether to stick with your plan or switch it up, talk about it with your trusted people. They can dish out advice and help you weigh the good and bad.

Make it a thing to give your plan a review regularly and check how far you've come. This can help you spot where you might need to fine-tune and keep you on the fast lane to your dream job.

Let's get down to the nitty-gritty with two scenarios: one where you might need to adjust your plan, and another where you might wanna hit the brakes.

Stick to Your Plan: Picture this - your dream is to be a pro illustrator, and one of your milestones was to hit up a summer art program in New York City to learn from the big guns. But then, whoosh! A global event hits, and the program's a no-go.

This is a hiccup, not a total show-stopper. It doesn't mean you should throw in the towel on your illustrator dream. Instead, you switch things up. Maybe you take an online class with a top artist or spend the summer beefing up your portfolio. You're still hustling toward your dream job, you're just taking a scenic detour to get there.

Time to Change Your Plan: Now, let's say you've been pouring your heart and soul into pursuing a career as a professional musician. You've practiced tirelessly, and performed at countless gigs, but deep down, something doesn't feel right. The spark you used to feel is fading, and you've discovered a passion for writing and storytelling.

It's time to reassess and shake things up. Maybe it's time to explore a career in writing or pursue a creative writing course. It's okay to let go of one dream if it no longer brings you joy and fulfillment. Sometimes, discovering new passions and following what truly excites you leads to a path that's even more rewarding in the long run.

Monitoring Your Progress

Setting out on your career quest feels like gearing up for an epic road trip. You've got your route and endpoint all planned out, but you know you have to keep your eyes peeled for those detour signs and maybe even flip the script if the situation calls for it. This means catching up with yourself regularly, taking a good, hard look at your plans, and possibly changing things up if the world throws you a curveball. Each baby step, no matter how small, is a win that edges you closer to your dream and gives you a motivational kick in the pants.

One of the best ways to track how far you've rolled and how much road you've still got ahead is by setting milestones as we mentioned earlier. Think of them as your road trip highlights, letting you know whether you're still cruising down the right freeway or if you need to take the next exit. And when you hit one? Break out the confetti. You've earned it!

Now, as you're road-tripping down your career path, remember all the gizmos you've got in your toolkit. There are a ton of digital assistants out there, from to-do list apps to spreadsheets, that can help you keep tabs on how you're doing. And why not make it visual with a progress chart? It can give you a snappy snapshot of how far you've come and the milestones you've already crushed. You'll find a whole list of tried and tested tools in the resources section of the book.

And finally, if you hit any speed bumps, don't sweat it. Challenges are just learning moments in disguise. Embrace them, adapt, and keep pushing in the direction you want to head. After all, every step, whether it's an uphill battle or a breezy downhill roll, gets you closer to your finish line.

Overcoming Obstacles and Setbacks

In your career quest, you're definitely going to run into obstacles and setbacks. Don't stress it - this is all part of the ride. Actually, how you handle these challenges can make the difference between totally nailing it and throwing in the towel. So, let's talk about how to spot potential roadblocks, whip up some strategies to take them on, and build some resilience to keep on cruising.

First up, think about what kind of problems might throw a wrench in your plans. It could be cash troubles, a lack of resources, or personal limitations. By spotting these speed bumps in advance, you can figure out how to leap over them or at least lessen their impact.

Next, you want to cultivate a problem-solving mindset. When a problem pops up, instead of freaking out or giving up, treat it like a riddle to solve. There's always more than one way to reach your goal, so mull over all your options. Don't be shy to ask for advice from your network and trusted guides, like mentors, teachers, or buddies. They might have a point of view you hadn't thought of.

Finally, let's talk about resilience. This is your power to bounce back when stuff hits the fan. To build up resilience, zoom in on what you can learn from each stumble. Keep a sunny outlook, and remember why you're so fired up about your goals in the first place. Throw yourself a party for every mini-win, and don't beat yourself up when stuff doesn't go the way you planned. It's important to look after your mental and emotional health, too. You might wanna try out mindfulness practices, like meditation or journaling, to help tackle stress and keep a clear mind.

In the end, by expecting challenges, preparing solutions early, and building resilience, you're arming yourself to handle any speed bump that comes your way. So, when setbacks come up, remember: they're just stepping stones on your journey to success.

As we wrap up this chapter, give yourself a massive high-five! You've powered through some seriously key steps – setting SMART goals, carving out a plan, tracking your progress, and learning to face obstacles head-on. Now, you have a blueprint that will lead you straight to your dream career. But remember, a plan is only as good as the action that powers it.

So, what's up next? The planning phase is just one slice of the pie. Now comes the real action - bringing the plan to life. This is where we get our hands dirty and get down to business. But don't worry, you're not going solo. I'll be right there with you, guiding you every step of the way.

In the next part of the book, we'll dive into some key skills you need to perfectly execute your plan. These aren't just any skills; these are the tools that will empower you to breathe life into your plan, navigate challenges, and snatch up opportunities that roll your way.

From CV and resume writing to totally smashing those interviews, we'll deep-dive into each of these skills, breaking them down into bite-sized pieces and serving up some actionable tips you can start using straight away. As we jump into this next part of your journey, remember that you're not just learning skills for your career, but also for life.

So, are you psyched to turn your plan into reality and take a giant leap closer to your dream career? Let's plunge into the next part: Bringing the Plan to Life - Essential Skills You Need to Nail Your Plan. Onwards and upwards!

We Hope You Enjoyed Part 1!

W e hope you've been enjoying Part 1 of The Essential Career Planning Handbook for Teens, discovering valuable insights and strategies for navigating the world of career planning. If you're finding the book helpful and insightful, we kindly request your support in leaving a quick review. Just a minute of your time can make a significant difference!

Customer reviews

★★★★☆ 4.7 out of 5

221 global ratings

5 star		76%
4 star		20%
3 star		3%
2 star		1%
1 star		1%

⌄ How customer reviews and ratings work

Review this product

Share your thoughts with other customers

Write a customer review

Scan this QR code to leave a quick review and help the next generation prosper!

Your feedback is incredibly valuable, not only for us but also for other parents and educators seeking guidance on career planning for teens. By sharing your thoughts, you'll contribute to the growth and improvement of RaiseYouthRight. Our hope is that with the information we share, we can make the next generation healthier, wealthier, and happier than ours!

We appreciate your support and look forward to diving into Part 2, where we'll explore practical ways to apply these valuable career planning tools.

II

Bringing the Plan to Life - Essential Skills to Smash Your Career Goal

Chapter 7 - Acing Applications, Resumes and Cover Letters

"Your work is going to fill a large part of your life, and the only way to be truly satisfied is to do what you believe is great work." - Steve Jobs

R eady to step up your game in the job market? Let's dive into one of the key tools you'll need: a stunning CV or resume. These are like your professional highlight reels - they show off what you've got to offer in terms of skills, experiences, and achievements.

Whether you're applying for your first part-time gig or gearing up for a serious internship, a well-crafted CV or resume is your ticket to standing out from the crowd. These docs are more than just a list of what you've done; they show you've got the organization and attention to detail that employers love to see. So, buckle up - we're about to deep dive into the world of CVs and resumes and show you how to make yours shine.

First off, let's clear up what these two things are. A CV, or Curriculum Vitae (fancy Latin for "course of life"), is like your professional autobiography. It lists everything you've done in your work and school life, from part-time jobs to academic awards. It's super detailed and can be several pages long. If you're aiming for a role in academia, research, or a high-level professional job, this is the way to go.

A resume, on the other hand, is like a highlight reel of your skills, education, and work experiences. It's short, sweet, and tailored to the job you're after. It usually stays within one or two pages. So if you're looking for a gig that matches your skills and experiences, a resume is your best bet.

Here's a quick comparison to make things clearer:

CV:

- It's like your professional autobiography.
- Includes everything you've done in school and work.
- Can be several pages long.
- Perfect for academic, research, or high-level professional jobs.

Resume:

- Like a highlight reel of your skills, education, and work experiences.
- Short and tailored to the job you're applying for.
- Usually one or two pages long.

Let's say you're applying for a research internship at a big-time university. Here, a CV would be the best choice to show off your academic accomplishments and research projects. But if you're applying for a part-time gig at your favorite coffee shop, a resume would do the trick, showing off your customer service skills and relevant work experiences.

Now that we've cleared up the difference between a CV and a resume, you're ready to put your best foot forward. With the right document in hand, you'll be set to make a great impression and snag that job you've been eyeing.

Crack the CV Code: Action-Packed Writing, Keyword Mastery, and Tailored Triumphs

Ready to give your CV some oomph? We're here with some wicked tips to take your CV from "meh" to "marvelous!", showcasing your talents, experiences, and all the awesome stuff you've accomplished. We're not just talking basic advice; this is like the secret recipe for a standout CV.

1. **Be an Action Hero:** Remember that old English teacher who kept telling you to use strong, active verbs? They were onto something. Adding action verbs to your CV can make your achievements shine and show that you're a mover and shaker. Check out these action verbs to kick things off:

- Managed
- Developed
- Coordinated
- Analyzed
- Implemented
- Directed
- Streamlined
- Negotiated
- Evaluated
- Innovated

So, instead of saying, "I was in charge of planning events," you could say, "Coordinated and executed sponsor events, boosting attendance by 20%." Sounds way cooler, right?

2. **Master the Keyword Game**: When you're reading the job description, some words or phrases will pop up more than once. These are keywords, and they're

like a secret handshake between you and the potential employer. Slipping these keywords into your CV says, "I speak your language, and I've got the skills you need." Plus, many companies use special software (Application Tracking Systems, which we'll get into later, promise!) that searches for these keywords to sort CVs, so using them could give your CV a free pass to the next round.

For instance, if you're shooting for a software development job, you might see keywords like "Java," "Agile methodology," or "front-end development." So, when you're writing about your experiences, you might say, "Worked in a dynamic Agile team to develop Java-based applications, boosting system efficiency by 15%."

3. **Tailor Your CV:** It might seem like a good idea to use the same CV for every job you apply for, but here's the scoop – each job is unique, and your CV should mirror that. Customizing your CV for each job can really show an employer that you're the perfect fit.

Imagine you've been gunning for content writer jobs, but now you're keen on a social media management role. You'll want to tweak your CV to spotlight any social media experience and brag about your social media chops. Don't forget to include any relevant courses or certifications, and use numbers to prove your successes, like, "Managed social media channels for a local charity, increasing followers by a whopping 30% with targeted marketing campaigns."

Armed with these tips, you're all set to whip up a CV that stands out from the crowd, shines a spotlight on your talents and experiences, and makes you a top contender for your dream job.

Looks Matter: Making Your CV Shine with Great Fonts, Layout, and Design

It's time to unleash your creativity and make your CV stand out in the crowd. We're about to spill the beans on some awesome tricks to make your CV look totally on point.

Fonts: Choosing the right font is like picking the perfect outfit for a job interview. You wanna look professional and easy to understand, right? Well, the same goes for your CV! Stick with clean and easy-to-read fonts like Arial, Calibri, or Times New Roman. Avoid fancy or hard-to-read fonts that could make your CV a hot mess. And don't forget about font size! Keep the main text between 10 and 12 points and make headings a bit bigger.

Feeling trendy? Give Calibri size 11 a go for the main text and size 14 for headings.

Layout: Think of your CV's layout as a roadmap that guides the reader's eyes through your amazing achievements. Use clear headings and bullet points to break up big chunks of text. And don't forget about that magical thing called white space! Leave enough space between sections to make your CV super easy to read. Oh, and consistency is key! Keep the layout the same throughout the document, from headings to bullet points and spacing.

Divide your CV into neat sections like "Summary," "Education," "Experience," and "Skills." Use bold headings and bullet points to show off your awesomeness in each section.

Design Elements: Want to add a bit of pizzazz to your CV? Go for it! Adding some design flair can make your CV pop. Try using lines or borders to separate sections or add a splash of color to your headings. But remember, you're not creating a masterpiece here. The focus should be on your achievements and skills, not on how many colors you can fit on one page.

Let's say you're applying for a graphic design job. Sprinkle some color on your headings or use a sleek border to show off your creative side. But if you're going for a job in a more traditional field like finance, keep it classy with a simple black-and-white design, clean lines, and minimal design elements.

By paying attention to fonts, layout, and design, you can create a CV that not only tells your amazing story but also looks incredible. Just remember, finding the right balance between a professional look and a touch of your personal style is key. After all, your CV is all about YOU!

The Final Polish: Making Your CV Shine by Banishing Errors

You've just finished writing your CV or resume. Fantastic! But hold on a second, we're not done yet. We've got to make sure it's as perfect as can be, with no typos, grammar mistakes, or other hiccups that could put off potential employers. Don't worry, it's not as tough as it sounds. Just follow these 5 tips to make your CV or resume spotless every time:

1. **Take a Break**: Just finished your CV? Now, push your chair back, stand up, and take a little break. Doing something else for a while helps your brain reset, so when you come back to your CV, you'll be able to spot any mistakes more easily. You could take a walk, watch a funny YouTube video, or grab a quick snack. Once you're refreshed, it's time to dive back in and start proofreading.

2. **Read it Out Loud**: This might seem weird, but trust me, it works! Reading your CV out loud helps you catch awkward sentences or phrases that you might not notice when you read silently. Find a quiet spot and read your CV aloud, listening for anything that sounds off. If it doesn't sound right to you, chances are it won't sound right to the person reading it either.

3. **Spellcheck and Grammar Tools**: Don't forget to use the spell check feature in your word processing program, and tools like Grammarly can help you catch any grammar slip-ups. Remember, these tools aren't perfect and can't replace a good old-fashioned proofread, but they're a great starting point.

4. **Print it Out**: This might sound old-school, but it's super helpful. When you read on paper, you use a different part of your brain than when you read on a screen, which can help you spot mistakes you might have missed. Print out your CV, grab a pen or highlighter, and start scanning for any changes you need to make.

5. **Ask for a Second Opinion**: Got a friend, family member, or mentor who's really good at this stuff? Ask them to take a look at your CV. They might catch something you didn't, or have some great advice on how to make your CV even better. If you can, try to find someone who works in the field you're interested in - they'll know exactly what employers are looking for.

By spending a little extra time proofreading and editing, you'll make sure your CV or resume is a polished gem that's free of errors. Remember, this is your first impression of potential employers, so let's make it a great one!

The Role of References: When and How to Include References in a CV or Resume, and Selecting Appropriate Referees.

References are like your secret weapon, shining a light on how awesome you are and making employers go, "Wow!"

So, when should you include references?: It's best to save that space for your killer skills and achievements. Most employers will ask for references separately when they need them. So, don't stress about cramming them into your CV.

But hold on, we're not done yet! You still need to be prepared with some amazing referees. These are people who can vouch for your awesomeness and speak to your skills, work ethic, and character.

When choosing your referees, think about people who know you well in a professional or academic setting. It could be a teacher, a mentor, a coach, or a supervisor from a part-time job. Make sure to ask their permission first and let them know you'll be putting them down as a reference. You want to make sure they're ready to sing your praises when the time comes!

And don't forget to provide your referees with a heads-up when you start applying for jobs. That way, they'll be prepared if a potential employer reaches out to them.

So, remember, save space in your CV for your impressive skills and achievements. But always be ready with a list of awesome referees who can back you up and show employers just how amazing you are.

Mastering the Application Process

Even if your CV is in tip-top shape and you have glowing references, navigating the application process can be a bit of a maze. It's not just about sending out your CV or resume and hoping for the best. There's a lot more to consider like deadlines, necessary documents, essays, recommendation letters, and other ways to stand out.

1. **Deadlines**: These are super important. You've got to keep track of when each application is due. Missing a deadline can mean missing out on a great opportunity. So, create a schedule, set reminders on your phone, stick post-it notes all over your room, do whatever it takes to stay on top of those deadlines!

2. **Necessary Documents**: Apart from your CV or resume, you might need to provide other documents. This could include your academic transcripts, certifications, or even your passport for identity verification. Make sure you have these documents ready and in order.

3. **Essays**: Some jobs might ask you to write an essay as part of the application. This could be about why you're interested in the job, what you can bring to the company, or how you've overcome challenges. When writing these essays, be honest, be enthusiastic, and most importantly, be yourself. Show them what makes you, you!

4. **Recommendation Letters**: Some places might ask for recommendation letters (basically a more detailed version of a reference). These are usually from people who can vouch for your skills, character, and work ethic, like teachers or previous employers. Remember, it's polite to give people plenty of time to write these letters, so ask them well in advance.

5. **Stand Out**: With so many applications, you need to find ways to stand out. This could be through a unique cover letter (which we'll talk about soon), a portfolio showcasing your work, or even a creative CV or resume design. Just remember to stay professional and relevant to the job you're applying for.

6. **Bonus Tips:** Here are a few extra tips for you:

- Do Your Research: Show that you know about the company and role you're applying for. This can impress employers.
- Be Honest: Never lie on your application. It's not worth it and trust me, the truth usually comes out eventually.
- Follow Instructions: If they ask for a PDF, send a PDF. If they ask you to fill out an online form, fill it out. It shows you can follow instructions and are serious about the application.

With these tips in mind, you're ready to master the application process and navigate your way to your dream job. Remember, it's all about being organized, being prepared, and being yourself.

Applicant Tracking Systems (ATS): A Deep Dive and How to Make Your Resume Shine

Welcome to the world of job hunting, where understanding something called Applicant Tracking Systems (ATS) is super important. Lots of companies use these fancy bits of software to sift through mountains of resumes and find the best people for their jobs. Here's the lowdown on ATS and tips on making your resume a winner.

So, what's an ATS? Think of Applicant Tracking Systems like a helpful robot friend for recruiters. They scan your resume, looking for certain words and phrases that match the job description. They then give candidates a score based on how well their resumes match what the job is asking for. The higher your score, the better your chances of getting an interview!

Here are some of the best ways you can show the ATS you're the right guy or gal for the job:

Keywords are your new best friend: To make your resume ATS-ready, you need to hunt for the most important words and phrases in the job description and sprinkle them through your resume. Be sure to use the exact words from the job posting, or the ATS might not recognize them. Like, if the job wants "project management" experience, use the phrase "project management" in your resume, not "managing projects."

Keep it simple: When designing your resume, think clean and easy. ATS like simple layouts and can get confused by images, tables, columns, or text boxes. Stick to easy-to-read fonts like Arial, Calibri, or Times New Roman, and keep the style consistent throughout.

File format matters: Save your resume in a file format that's ATS-friendly, like Microsoft Word (.doc or .docx) or plain text (.txt). PDF files can sometimes confuse ATS, so it's best to avoid them.

Customize, customize, customize: This tip is so important, it's worth saying three times! Always tailor your resume to each job you apply for. Make sure the keywords and phrases you use match the specific job posting. This not only helps you get past the ATS but also shows the company you're really interested in the job.

Use keywords but don't go crazy with them: While keywords are important, don't go over the top. ATS are smart and can tell when a resume is stuffed full of keywords in a way that doesn't make sense. Focus on adding keywords naturally, showcasing your skills and experience.

By getting to know Applicant Tracking Systems and using these tips, you can make your resume shine for ATS and boost your chances of making it to the interview stage. Remember, a well-crafted, easy-to-read, job-specific resume is your ticket to landing your dream job.

Cover Letters Decoded: What are They and How to Make Yours Pop!

Want to really impress potential employers and stand out from the crowd? A killer cover letter just might be what you're looking for. This one-page document tags along with your resume and introduces you to your future employer. It's your chance to say "Hey, this is me, this is why I'm perfect for this job, and here's a little glimpse into who I am." Picture it as your personal elevator pitch!

Ready to craft a cover letter that'll make employers sit up and take notice? Here's how:

1. **Custom-made goodness**: Tailor-make your cover letter for each job you apply for. Do a little detective work on the company and the role you're eyeing, then show how your skills, experience, and values match up with the job and the vibe of the company. Say you're applying for a marketing gig at a company that's all about the environment. Talk about your love for green living and any related projects or volunteering you've done.

2. **Tell a story:** Grab the reader's attention by sharing a story that showcases your skills and achievements. It's a surefire way to be remembered and to make a connection with the job. Applying for a customer service job? Share a tale about how you went above and beyond to help a customer at your last job.

3. **Be yourself:** Let your personality shine in your cover letter! Keep the tone friendly and real. It'll help the hiring manager get a sense of who you are and how you'd gel with their team.

4. **Keep it snappy:** When it comes to cover letters, less is more. Aim for three or four short paragraphs that cover the basics – who you are, why you're a good fit for the job, and what you bring to the job.

5. **Error-free zone:** No one likes typos or grammar mistakes, especially hiring managers. Just like your resume, your cover letter needs to be spotless. Proofread it carefully, and get a friend or family member to give it a once-over, too.

Your cover letter is your chance to show off your skills and personality, so make it count! Be fearless and let your awesomeness take center stage!

Going Digital: How to Rock a Modern CV and Personal Brand Online

In our hyper-connected world, having an online presence is no longer a "nice-to-have" – it's a must-have. And your personal brand? Well, it's your secret weapon in your quest to land that dream job. A kick-butt personal brand sets you apart from the pack, lets your unique skills and personality shine, and shows potential employers that you mean business. Plus, it could be your golden ticket to opportunities you never even knew existed!

Your LinkedIn Profile Matters!

If you're a job seeker, there's one place you've gotta be, it's LinkedIn. This professional networking hotspot is like the ultimate career fair that's open 24/7, and it's packed with potential employers looking for someone just like you. So, what's the secret to a winning LinkedIn profile? Let's break it down.

First off, keep your profile fresh and updated. Snap a crisp, professional photo (think friendly and approachable!), craft a catchy headline that sums up who you are and what you're about, and pen a summary that spotlights your superpowers. And don't be shy about sharing your work history, education, and the skills you bring to the table. Oh, and remember, LinkedIn is all about making connections (we'll dive deeper into this in Chapter 9). So, start linking up with others in your industry, join conversations in groups, and post content that adds value to your network.

Let's imagine you're Sarah Smith, a college student studying marketing. Here's how she might rock her LinkedIn profile:

Professional pic: A high-res, well-lit selfie where Sarah's dressed to impress and flashing a friendly smile, against a distraction-free backdrop.

Headline: "Future Marketing Maven | Earning a B.S. in Marketing at XYZ University | Crazy about Brand Strategy & Social Media"

Summary: "I'm a marketing enthusiast studying at XYZ University, chasing after my Bachelor's degree in Marketing. I'm a brand strategy and social media buff, and I've gotten my hands dirty managing social accounts for a local charity. Always hungry to learn and grow, I'm on the lookout for internships and networking opportunities to supercharge my marketing prowess."

Work history: Sarah would share her relevant internships, part-time gigs, or volunteer roles, showcasing what she achieved and the skills she honed.

Education: Sarah would list her current uni, her major, and when she's set to graduate, plus any coursework or projects that are worth a shout-out.

Skills: Sarah would flaunt her relevant skills, like managing social media, crafting content, conducting market research, and analyzing data.

Now, it's your turn to create a LinkedIn profile that's just as awesome. So, go ahead, get your LinkedIn game on, and start making those connections! To learn more about best practices for LinkedIn networking, be sure to check out this section in the networking chapter.

TikTok and Instagram Resumes: The Next Cool Thing in Job Hunting?

Heard of TikTok and Instagram, right? Sure, you have! But did you know that they're not just for awesome dance challenges or perfect selfie moments? Now you can use them to land your dream job too! Yes, we're talking video resumes, a super cool and creative way to show off your skills, achievements, and personality to future employers.

So, TikTok has a program called "TikTok Resumes." Their goal? To make TikTok a go-to place for job hunters like you. Now, the folks at Hubspot decided to find out what professionals think about these video resumes. They asked 98 marketing pros, and guess what? 68% of them said they've considered a candidate with a TikTok or Instagram resume!

But here's the thing. While some people think these video resumes are unique, fun, and a great way to show off your creativity, others still prefer the good old traditional resume. So, it seems like these video resumes might work best as an extra, not as a complete replacement for a regular resume.

Want to give it a go? Here's how:

Keep it Short and Sweet: TikTok videos usually last 15 to 60 seconds, so get your best stuff out there quick!

Start with a Splash: Open your video with something really cool that'll make people want to see more.

Show off Your Wins: Talk about your best achievements and skills. You know, the ones that make you perfect for the job.

Get Creative: TikTok and Instagram are all about fun, so use those editing tools, effects, and catchy tunes to make your video pop! But remember, keep it professional too.

Wrap it up Right: End your video by telling viewers where they can find more about you, like your LinkedIn profile or personal website.

Just one thing, though. Always remember to read the job posting super carefully.

If they ask for a traditional resume and cover letter, make sure you send those in, even if you also share a video resume. Do some detective work on the company to make sure your video fits in with what they're all about.

Building Your Own Online Resume/Portfolio Website

Ever dreamed of owning your own slice of the internet? A place where you can show off your resume, your work portfolio, and all the amazing things you've done? It's a game-changer, especially if you're into the creative arts like design, writing, or photography. Imagine having a 24/7 online showcase of your top-notch work!

Start by choosing a neat, professional design, and ensure your contact info, a mini-bio, and samples of your work are easy to spot.

Ready to turn your online resume or portfolio website into a masterpiece? Let's talk about best practices:

Claim Your Territory: First off, snag a custom domain name. Keep it simple and professional - ideally, it's your own name (like www.yourname.com). It's not only super slick, but it also makes it easy for potential employers or clients to find you online.

Simplicity is Key: Make your website a joy to navigate with clear menus and categories. This way, visitors can zip straight to the info they want about you and your killer work.

Fan Club: Why not include some stellar testimonials or references from teachers, mentors, or past bosses? It's like your very own cheerleading team shouting your praises to the world.

Write On!: Fancy starting a blog or penning articles on topics you're passionate about? It's an awesome way to flaunt your knowledge, passion, and communication skills. Plus, it might help your website climb up the search engine ranks.

Bragging Rights: Don't be shy about boasting about any awards or recognitions you've scooped. It's your stage - so strut your stuff!

Get Linked: Connect your website to your LinkedIn profile and any other social media or professional platforms where you're displaying your work.

Stay Fresh: Keep your website buzzing with your latest projects and experiences. It shows you're always on the move and continually growing.

Mobile Friendly: Make sure your website shines and functions perfectly on smartphones and tablets, because loads of people will browse it on their mobile devices.

Call Me Maybe?: Make it super simple for visitors to reach out to you. Add a contact form, your email address, or phone number, and invite them to drop you a line.

By weaving these elements into your online resume or portfolio website, you're creating more than just a webpage. You're crafting a powerful platform that puts your skills, experiences, and potential under the spotlight.

Social Media: Your Digital Footprint

Ever thought about the fact that your future boss might be checking out your Instagram or reading your tweets? Yep, they could be doing a deep dive into your social media profiles right now. It's vital to make sure your profiles are looking their best, all up-to-date, and showcasing all the awesome stuff you're doing and achieving. You can use platforms like Twitter and Instagram to share cool industry info, make connections with industry professionals, and show off what a whizz you are in your field.

So how do you make your social media game strong? Start with a privacy check. Decide who you want to see your posts, maybe you want to keep your goofy selfies and pet pics separate from your professional profile. Next, choose a profile picture that looks professional and clear. A high-quality shot of you looking friendly is perfect for platforms like LinkedIn and Twitter.

When it comes to your bio, make it catchy and informative. Talk about what you're into, your big wins, and your career dreams. And don't forget to use keywords that relate to your field, that way people can find you more easily.

Sharing is caring, right? Post articles, news, and resources that relate to your field. It's a super way to show off your passion and knowledge. And remember to be social on social media! Like, comment on, and share other people's posts. It's a fantastic way to start conversations and make connections.

Hashtags are like the yellow brick road that leads people to your content. Use relevant ones to get your posts seen by more people. And make sure you're giving off a consistent vibe across all your profiles. Using the same colors, fonts, and styles can help create a personal brand.

Don't be shy about posting your wins, like awards, special projects, or times when you've volunteered. It's a great way to show off your commitment and skills. And don't forget to join online groups or communities that share your interests. It's a fabulous way to stay updated about the latest trends and opportunities.

And one last thing, do a quick search of your name on Google from time to time. Make sure your social media profiles are giving off the right vibes. But don't go crazy and Google yourself every single day, okay? Cool!

Building a rock-solid, professional online presence is key in today's job-hunting world. Your resume is more than just a piece of paper; it's a combination of your social media profiles and your personal brand. Making sure your online profiles are up-to-date and engaging can boost your credibility and grab the attention of potential employers. The digital world is your oyster, full of opportunities to show off your skills, knowledge, and achievements. So, use it to help you land your dream job!

As you start pulling together your modern resume and boosting your online presence, remember that interviews are a big part of the journey. In the next chapter, we're going to deep dive into the world of interviewing and help you ace those conversations to get you through the door to your dream job!

Chapter 8 - Nailing the Interviews

"Believe in yourself and all that you are. Know that there is something inside you that is greater than any obstacle." - Christian D. Larson

S o you've crafted an A-grade resume, nailed your cover letter, and piqued the interest of potential employers or college admissions folks. Now, the butterflies are starting to flutter in your belly, because it's time for the big kahuna: the interview.

Breathe in, breathe out! Yes, interviews are pretty big potatoes, but hey, they're just your personal catwalk to strut your awesome personality and skillset.

But why all the fuss about interviews, you ask? Here's the scoop. Whether you're aiming for internships, part-time gigs, full-ride college admissions, or those fancy full-time jobs, interviews are like the secret password. They let the interviewers decide if you're the right puzzle piece for their team, school, or company. And for you? It's the perfect platform to let your passion and enthusiasm do a little happy dance.

Imagine you're eyeing an internship or part-time work. The interview is your prospective employer's chance to check if you can juggle the job along with school. Remember, these gigs are your sneak peek into your dream industry, so it's key to bring your A-game and come prepared.

For college admissions? Interviews add a personal splash of color to your application, giving you the chance to chat about your dreams, experiences, and victories in a more intimate setting. Not all colleges require interviews, but if the chance arises, seize it! It's like a power-up for your application.

And when it comes to full-time job applications? Interviews are the main act, the spotlight moment for employers to weigh up if you've got the goods to thrive in their company. This is your chance to convince them that you're the superstar they've been looking for, so be sure to rock it out.

No matter the type of interview on your horizon, remember, come armed with preparation, ooze confidence, and stay true to your authentic self – and you'll totally crush it.

To ensure you're thoroughly prepared, it's crucial to investigate the company or college you're applying to, comprehend the role or program you're targeting, and rehearse interview questions suitable for your age group. Believe me, you'll pat yourself on the back later for putting in the hard yards!

Research: The Secret Weapon to Winning the Interview Game

Get ready to level up your interview game! They say knowledge is power and boy, are they right. When it comes to crushing your interview, being prepared is everything. It's not just about knowing the basics of the company or college you're interviewing with. It's about diving deep into the details and understanding what you're up against.

First things first, let's talk about different interview formats. You might come across phone interviews, video interviews, or in-person interviews.

Each one has its quirks and tricks to master. For video interviews, make sure your tech is on point and glitch-free. And when facing a panel interview, keep your cool and show off your awesome skills. Quick online searches can give you the inside scoop on what to expect and how to prep.

Now, let's dig into getting to know your potential future home, whether it's a cool company or an awesome college. It's not just about memorizing their mission statement (yawn!). You want to show genuine interest in their values and culture. Start by exploring their website – it's like a treasure trove of information. Check out their "About Us" and "News" sections to uncover juicy insights about their history, achievements, and what makes them unique.

But wait, there's more! Don't forget to stalk them on social media too. Check out their Facebook, Twitter, Instagram, and LinkedIn pages. See what they're posting, how they engage with their audience, and any recent updates. And here's a pro tip: dig deeper by searching for news articles or press releases about the company or college. This will keep you up to date on their latest accomplishments and initiatives. And while you're at it, get to know their industry landscape, trends, and even their competitors. Trust me, it'll impress your interviewers.

Now, let's zoom in on the role or program you're aiming for. Whether it's an internship, part-time job, major, or joining a cool club or team, you need to know what you're getting into. Read the job or program description like it's your secret map to success. Pay attention to the responsibilities, the qualities they're looking for, and the skills they value. Highlight or jot down the important stuff.

Ready to play detective? Start by researching similar roles or programs online. This will give you a sense of what's expected. Then, reflect on your own skills, experiences, and achievements that align with the role. Remember those times when you showed off your skills like a boss. Those stories will impress your interviewers and make you stand out from the crowd.

Now that you're armed with all this knowledge, it's time to prepare your own set of questions. Show them you're serious and ready to make an impact from day one. Ask about the day-to-day tasks, the challenges you might face, and opportunities for growth. And don't forget to ask about their company or program culture – it shows you're interested in being a part of their awesome team.

With your research done and questions in hand, you're unstoppable! Remember, your interview is your time to shine. Be confident, be yourself, and let your passion for the opportunity shine through.

Practice Makes Perfect

Practicing may seem like a total drag, but believe me, it's super important for upping your confidence and making sure you crush it in the interview. You can ask a parent, a friend, or a teacher to step in as the interviewer and toss some probable questions at you.

For example, if you're aiming for an internship or part-time gig, imagine how you'd answer a question like "What made you go for this job?" or "How do you balance school with all your other stuff?" If it's a college admissions interview, prepare to discuss your favorite classes, what you love to do after school, and why that specific college makes your heart skip a beat.

The more you practice, the more cool and composed you'll be when the spotlight's on you. So, take a deep breath, get your practice game strong, and always keep in mind - you're totally equipped to rock this!

Common Interview Questions and How to Answer Them

Here are a few common interview questions, with some tips to handle them like a boss.

Q. Tell me about yourself.

This one seems simple, right? But it's a bit of a curveball because it's so broad. They're trying to get a feel for who you are, so share a quick snapshot of your life story, what you're into, and what sets you apart. Talk up your strong points, school wins, and any side activities that link with the role or program. Remember to keep it relevant to the program you're interviewing for.

Q. What are your future goals?

Interviewers often want to hear about your future dreams to grasp your drive and ambition. Consider your short-term and long-term goals linked with your education, career, and personal development. It's cool if you're not sure about every detail – just show you've got your eye on the future and you're open to exploring new paths.

Q. Why are you interested in this opportunity?

This is your moment to show your excitement and explain why you're the perfect fit for the role or program. Speak about what stokes your enthusiasm about the chance and how it matches your interests, goals, or values. Ensure you've done your homework on the company or college so you can drop in specific details that caught your interest.

Q. How do you handle stress or challenging situations?

Let's face it, we all bump into stress and challenges, and interviewers want to see how you manage these hurdles. Share a real-life example of a tough spot you've faced (it could be school-related or personal), and lay out how you tackled it. Show you can stay chill under pressure, solve problems, and learn from your adventures. Be sure to talk about the lessons you learned from the experience.

Q. Can you tell me about a time you worked as part of a team?

Working in a team is a big deal in many settings, so they want to know how you gel with others. Share a moment from school, your extra activities, or even a personal project where you worked with a group. Talk about your role, what you brought to the table, and any group hurdles you conquered together.

Q. What is your biggest strength?

When answering this one, consider a quality or skill that makes you stand out and is relevant to the opportunity you're chasing. Be honest, but don't shy away from showing off a bit! Share a specific example of how you've shown this strength, whether it's in school, your activities, or personal projects. This will help them understand how your strong suit can drive success in the role or program.

For example, you might say, "One of my biggest strengths is being an effective communicator. Being part of the debate club at school helped me build solid public speaking skills and the ability to share my thoughts clearly. I believe this skill will be handy in team collaborations and pitching my ideas in the role."

Q. What is your biggest weakness?

This one's a bit of a tough one. The trick here is, to be honest about a weakness while showing you're actively working on it. You don't want to admit a weakness that could be a deal-breaker, but you also don't want to give a generic answer that feels insincere.

Instead, choose a weakness that's real but not a game-changer for the opportunity, and explain how you're taking steps to beat it. For instance, you could say, "I'm trying to level up my time management. Sometimes, I struggle with setting priorities when I've got a lot on my plate. But, I've started using a planner to keep my schedule tidy and set deadlines, which has helped me become more punctual and focused."

Q: How do you plan to juggle school and work?

Remember that they're likely asking about your ability to balance school and work because they want to ensure you can handle the workload and ace both areas. They're not out to trick you; they genuinely want to grasp how you'll handle everything.

To prepare for this one, consider your current schedule and any strategies you use to keep your time in check. Reflect on how you've successfully juggled multiple commitments in the past, like school projects, extra activities, or even part-time gigs. This will arm you with specific examples for the interview.

When you tackle this question, be frank about your priorities. You could say something like, "I know balancing school and work can be a bit of a tightrope walk, but I'm ready to give my best in both areas. I've successfully handled multiple extra activities alongside my schoolwork before, so I'm confident in my ability to manage the workload. I prioritize my tasks based on deadlines and importance, and I use a planner to keep me organized and on point."

(Hint: To best prepare for this question be sure to check out Chapter 13)

Remember, when answering interview questions, take a deep breath, and let your real personality shine. Don't be afraid to let your excitement and passion come through. Rehearse your replies ahead of time, but don't just memorize them – you want to sound natural and real.

Don't forget to peek at the resources chapter for a more comprehensive list of interview questions to rehearse! You've got this!

Dressing for Success

You might be thinking, "Why does what I wear to an interview even matter?" But believe me, what you rock up in can be a game-changer. Your outfit is kind of like your first hello, and you want to make sure it's a top-notch one. So, here are some pointers on picking out the right interview gear for teens, considering your age and the type of gig or school you're after.

First up, you've got to figure out what the vibe is at the place you're inter-viewing. Is it a laid-back setting, like a summer camp or your neighborhood café? Or is it on the more formal side, like a law office or a high-end college? The trick here is to dress just a notch above the usual attire. If you're in doubt, it's always safer to lean towards looking more professional.

For a chill environment, think about going with neat jeans or khakis teamed up with a button-down shirt or a blouse. You can also add a cardigan or blazer to up the smartness factor of your outfit. Steer clear of anything too tight, too short, or plastered with controversial slogans or images. Remember, you want to come off as taking this chance seriously!

If you're interviewing for a more formal place, it's time to crank up your wardrobe a notch. For guys, this might mean getting into dress pants, a button-down shirt, and a tie, or even a suit if you've got one. For gals, consider rocking a professional dress, a skirt and blouse combo, or a pantsuit.

And don't forget about your shoes – make sure they're neat and tidy!

Now, let's move on to the finer details. Looking neat and tidy is super essential, so ensure your hair is on point, your nails are clean, and your clothes are iron-free. If you wear makeup, keep it low-key and natural. When it comes to accessories, stick to something classic and subtle – you don't want anything too glitzy or distracting.

At the end of the day, the most crucial part is feeling confident and comfy in your interview attire. When you look fab, you feel fab, and that confidence will sparkle during your interview. So, take some time to plot out your wardrobe game plan, and remember that dressing for success is just another way to prove that you're the ideal candidate for the opportunity!

Mastering the Post-Interview Follow-Up

Let's be real – once the nerve-wracking interview is over, the sigh of relief is pretty much audible. But wait, your job isn't quite done yet. There's still one final, crucial step left – acing the follow-up game!

Picture this: Your interview went super well. The conversation flowed, you nailed those tricky questions, and you managed to paint a fantastic image of what an absolute rockstar you'd be for the role. But it doesn't stop there. You want to leave an enduring impression, one that'll make your interviewers think, "Wow, they were not just awesome but also super considerate!"

This is where the follow-up etiquette, especially the good old thank-you note, comes into play. It's like the cherry on top of a successful interview sundae. A timely and well-written thank-you note is more than just good manners – it demonstrates your professionalism, your genuine interest in the role, and the respect you hold for the interviewer's time.

So, what goes into this magical note, you ask? Here are the top tips to up your follow-up game:

Timing is everything: Aim to send your thank-you note within 24 hours after the interview. You're still fresh in their minds, and it shows you're on top of your game.

Choose your medium wisely: Email is usually your safest bet – it's quick, and professional, and most people check their inboxes regularly. If you have a physical address and the vibe feels right, a handwritten note can add a personal touch.

Keep it short and sweet: This isn't the time to pen down an essay. Keep it concise, friendly, and genuine.

What to include: Thank your interviewer for their time, mention a specific topic you enjoyed discussing, reiterate your interest in the role, and let them know you're looking forward to hearing from them.

Remember, this follow-up note is your final chance to make an impression, so make it count. Nail this last step, and you're officially a complete interview whizz – well done, you!

Keeping Your Cool: Taming Those Interview Butterflies

We've all been there – the sweaty palms, the jittery legs, and the pesky butterflies wreaking havoc in our stomachs. Interviews can send even the most seasoned of us into a frenzy of nerves. But hey, feeling a tad nervous is totally okay – it just shows you care! But remember, we don't want those nerves to steal your shine during the interview. So, let's talk about some chill-pill strategies to keep those jitters in check.

Breathwork is your best friend: Deep, controlled breathing can help slow your heart rate and relax your mind. A few minutes before your interview, find a quiet spot and take slow, deep breaths, focusing on your exhales. Trust us, it works wonders!

Preparation is the ultimate confidence booster: When you're armed with the right information about the company or college, the role or program you're applying for, and have responses ready for potential questions, you'll naturally feel more at ease. So, do your homework!

Practice to perfection: Much like your favorite dance move or basketball shot, the more you practice, the more comfortable you'll feel. Mock interviews can help you get used to the interview dynamics. Rope in a friend, family member, or even your trusty mirror for practice sessions!

Positive visualization: Athletes often use this technique to prep for a big game. Close your eyes, imagine walking into the interview room, shaking hands with confidence, nailing your responses, and leaving the room with a smile of satisfaction.

Move it, move it: Physical activity is a great stress-buster. If you have time, take a brisk walk or do some light exercises before your interview. It can help dissipate nervous energy.

Use the power of music: Listening to your favorite upbeat tunes can help boost your mood and confidence. So, put on your headphones, and let your favorite artist tune up your mood!

Stay hydrated and well-nourished: Eating a light, nutritious meal and staying hydrated can keep you feeling good and focused.

Mind your body language: Stand tall, smile, make eye contact, and offer a firm handshake. It's amazing how positive body language can make you feel more confident.

Remember, it's okay to not know everything: Interviewers understand that you're a student and don't expect you to know everything. It's okay to admit when you don't know something. Honesty is always appreciated!

Keep perspective: Lastly, remember, it's just an interview. It's not a life-or-death situation. Even if things don't go as planned, it's not the end of the world. Every interview is a learning experience.

So, go out there and charm the socks off your interviewers. You've got this!

Chapter 9 - Making Connections: Networking

"Your network is your net worth." – *Porter Gale*

B race yourselves because we're about to jump into a super crucial step in getting your career off the ground: networking. We're gonna start from scratch, cover the basics, and before you know it, you'll be building connections like a boss.

Imagine networking as the art of creating and nurturing relationships with folks who can give you valuable advice, help, support, and opportunities related to your career path. It's not just about gathering a pile of business cards or bulking up your LinkedIn connections; it's more about growing real, meaningful relationships that bring benefits for everyone involved.

7 Powerful Benefits of Networking for Your Career Success

You might find yourself asking, "Is networking really worth my time?" It's a valid question! Well, we've got seven, yes, seven reasons to convince you that networking can really kick your career into high gear.

1. **Unlocking the Secret Job Vault:** You won't believe this, but a lot of job openings never make it to the public job boards. They're filled up by people who know people. Networking is your secret handshake to this hidden world of jobs, connecting you to folks who have the lowdown on these secret openings.

2. **Learning from the School of Life:** By networking, you'll get to hear amazing stories and gain wisdom from people with all kinds of backgrounds and experiences. Think of it like a free ticket to a festival of career advice, knowledge, and insights!

3. **Building Your Very Own Cheer Squad:** Networking isn't just about finding jobs; it's also about finding your tribe. These are the folks who'll cheer you on, give you advice, and help you stay motivated on your career journey. It's like having your own personal team of superheroes!

4. **Exploring the Land of Opportunities**: Networking can open doors you didn't even know existed. Jobs, internships, mentorships, partnerships - you name it! The more people you connect with, the more chances you have to stumble upon something awesome.

5. **Boosting Your Cool Factor:** When you network, you get the chance to show off your smarts and skills to other professionals. Leaving a great impression on them can raise your reputation in the industry and might even lead to referrals.

6. **Leveling Up Your People Skills**: Networking is also a fantastic way to polish those important soft skills like conversation, active listening, and relationship building. These are skills that employers love, so consider networking as a fun training ground.

7. **Staying on Top of the Game:** Networking keeps you in the loop about what's hot and happening in your field. That way, you're always updated

on the latest trends, tech, and tricks of the trade, keeping you sharp and competitive.

Networking can be your secret weapon in this crazy career adventure, but you have to master the ground rules to really find your networking mojo.

Networking Etiquette: The Ground Rules

Before we jump into networking there are some unspoken rules we need to talk about. They're called networking etiquette and trust me, they're mega important. They'll help you make real friends (not just professional connections!) and show people that you're serious about your goals.

Rule 1: Be true to you

Whether you're typing on your keyboard or chatting face-to-face, always keep it real. Show interest in others, be genuine, and let your personality shine like a diamond. People dig it when you're honest and authentic, and they'll want to connect with you even more.

Rule 2: Listen up!

Don't just space out waiting for your turn to talk. Listen to what people are saying, ask questions that show you're curious, and try to see things from their point of view. It's like giving them a high-five with your ears!

Rule 3: Body language matters

Did you know your body can talk without saying a word? Keep eye contact, stand tall, and shake hands like a boss. It shows that you're confident and ready for anything.

Rule 4: Give first, and then take

Networking is like a see-saw. You can help others, and you can ask for help. It's all about balance. And remember, always try to give more than you take, and give before you take!

Rule 5: Get your elevator pitch ready

Imagine you've got just a few seconds in an elevator with someone to wow them with your career dreams. What would you say? That's your elevator pitch. Keep it ready to dazzle new people you meet.

Rule 6: Keep in touch

Met someone new? Send them a message to say thank you and that you'd like to keep the chat going. It's like a virtual fist bump!

Rule 7: Space, the final frontier

Networking isn't about pestering people. Respect their time, and don't be that person who floods their inbox with messages.

Rule 8: Stay organized

Keep track of the cool people you meet in a spreadsheet or an app. Write down their names, how you can reach them, and anything else you think is important. It'll help you remember who's who as you make more friends.

Rule 9: Say thanks

After you meet someone new, shoot them a quick message to say thanks and that you're excited about staying in touch.

Stick to these rules, and you'll be a networking ninja in no time. Remember, networking is about making real connections and being genuinely helpful. Keep that in your mind, and your network will start growing like magic!

Overcoming Networking Anxiety

If just the idea of networking makes your palms sweat and your heart perform a mini break dance of panic, know you're not the only one. It's totally normal to feel the networking nerves, especially when you're just stepping into this wild career jungle. But don't worry, we're here to help you turn this networking scare into a dare.

First things first, get ready to rock. Feeling prepared is a massive confidence booster. So, if there's a networking event on the horizon, prep it up. Do your homework about the companies or professionals you'll meet, rehearse your elevator pitch till it sounds awesome, and have some curious questions up your sleeve. Walk into that event like you own the place.

Let's get this straight - those pros with the fancy job titles, they're people just like you and me. Yep, they started from scratch too and they might even be feeling a bit jittery at times. So, be yourself, flash your best smile, and you'll find most folks are super happy to chat and share their journey.

Remember that networking isn't a trophy-hunting game for business cards. It's all about making genuine connections. So, chillax. No need to meet every single person in the room. Try having a couple of meaningful conversations where you really vibe with people.

And here's a secret weapon - listen. Listen like your life depends on it. When you're focused on the other person, your nerves take a back seat. Dive into what they're saying, ask questions that show you're really interested and engaged. Before you know it, you're more into the conversation than worried about your nerves.

If you're feeling like a bundle of nerves, it's cool to admit it. No one's expecting you to be a superhero. Being honest can actually kickstart a great conversation. Chances are others have been in your shoes and they might even share some handy tips or encouraging words.

Remember the old saying, practice makes perfect? It's true. The more you network, the better you get at it. So, go on and get your networking on. Join clubs, show up at events, and grab every opportunity to practice your skills.

And hey, don't forget to give yourself a well-deserved high-five after each networking event. Think about what you rocked and celebrate your wins, whether you made a cool new friend or overcame your fears. This will boost your confidence for your next networking challenge.

Try out these strategies, push your comfort zone a bit, and you'll find that networking gets easier and, dare I say, even enjoyable. Take a deep breath, and believe in your awesome self – you've totally got this!

How to Contribute to Your Network Even as a Student

Alright, let's debunk a myth. If you're a high school or college student, you might be thinking that you've got zilch to offer your network, especially when you're networking with those super-experienced professionals. But that couldn't be further from the truth!

With your fresh perspective, bucketloads of energy, and untapped potential that's itching to break free, you're a goldmine! So, let's take a look at how you can add some value to your network and make those connections as strong as superhero friendships.

Flaunt Your Skills: If you're a wizard at something like graphic design or can plan events like a pro, offer to lend a hand with a project. Your fresh views can be like a cool breeze on a hot day. So share your ideas.

Speak Up: Keeping the conversation going is key, so ask for advice, ping across updates, and show your thirst for learning. And remember, a simple 'thank you' can be like sunshine on a cloudy day. It shows your gratitude for their time and support.

Listen Up and Stay Engaged: Offer your listening ear, because sometimes, all someone needs is to be heard. Stay on top of the latest buzz in your mentor's industry, sharing any hot-off-the-press updates. This way, you're showing you're both interested and clued in.

Be their cheerleader on social media: Like, share, and comment on their posts. This gives them a digital boost and shows you're rooting for them. If you stumble upon a cool app or a handy resource, share the love. It's a nifty way to lend a hand and show your proactive side.

Join the Crew: Lend your skills to help or co-host events. It's a two-way street - you learn tons, and it proves you're committed to their success. Make introductions to widen their network by introducing them to your buddies or other professionals with similar interests.

Sharing is Caring: If you spot something they might find fascinating or useful, ping it over. It proves you're tuned in and eager to help. Celebrate their wins by shouting about their achievements on your networks. This gives them a profile boost and shows you're cheering them on.

Give Back: Got some free time? Volunteer for a project or organization they're involved in. It's an incredible experience for you and a big thumbs up for them. And lastly, if they're cool with it, offer some constructive feedback. It can help them level up and shows you're truly invested in their success. Just be sure your words are respectful and kind.

Armed with these tips, you're all set to make your network sparkle. Now let's get out there and find those all-important connections.

Making Friends and Connections Through School and Hobbies

You know those clubs, sports teams, or community service projects you're part of? They're not just a cool way to spend time or help others - they're also an awesome place to make connections. When you join in, you meet people who are into the same things as you. And these friendships can turn into important professional relationships down the line.

Your teachers, coaches, and club advisors are also a goldmine for networking. They're usually pretty plugged into their fields and can introduce you to other pros or give you useful advice.

Plus, being part of these activities lets you show off your skills, like teamwork, leadership, and communication. Impress people with these, and they'll remember you when it's time to network.

Be sure to keep an eye out for events, competitions, or performances that involve other schools or groups. These are perfect chances to meet more people and make more connections for your future career.

If you didn't know this already, your school community is a hidden goldmine for networking opportunities! Let's start with your school's alumni network. Many schools have them and they're chock-full of people who were once in your shoes and have now hit it big in their careers. Don't be shy to give a shout-out to alumni who are rocking it in the field you're interested in. Ask them for their golden nuggets of wisdom or maybe even for an informational interview.

Now here's an idea you might not have considered: your classmates' parents! You never know who might be a secret superstar in a cool industry or who has a buddy that's just perfect for you to connect with. So go ahead and ask your pals to introduce you, or better yet, show up at events where the parents are hanging out.

Let's not forget the amazing resources right under your nose at school. The career center, your counselors, and your teachers can be like your own personal networking dream team. They're often brimming with advice and might even be able to hook you up with contacts at local businesses or organizations.

School events can also be a great avenue for networking. If there's a career fair or a guest speaker event, get yourself there pronto! It's the perfect place to put your friendly face on and start building those all-important connections. So what are you waiting for? Your school's networking opportunities are waiting for you!

Networking Through Volunteering and Community Involvement

Ready to make a real impact and cross paths with some awesome folks at the same time? Lending a hand and getting stuck into your local community can do just that. Seek out a non-profit or charity that gets your heart racing - maybe it's all about education, protecting our planet, or lending a hand to our furry friends. Once you join, you'll come across like-minded people who share your passion and might just become part of your network.

School clubs or groups are another epic spots to connect with people. Whether you're all about the student council, love a good debate, or live for the thrill of sports, these activities can link you up with classmates, teachers, and even pros in the field you're keen on.

Got a unique talent, like whipping up awesome designs, being a social media guru, or planning killer events? Why not lend your skills to local businesses or community groups? It's a total win-win - you get to beef up your professional portfolio and run into even more potential network connections.

And hey, remember, when you're out there volunteering or lending a hand, don't hold back about sharing your career dreams and aspirations. Tap into the wisdom of the folks you meet, ask all the questions, and always remember to catch up after an event or project.

Networking through giving back is all about keeping it real, staying tuned in, and being open to soaking up wisdom from others. Stick to this, and you'll be forging meaningful connections that'll be with you all the way to your dream job.

Becoming a LinkedIn Pro: Growing Your Network and Shining Online

Alright, you've definitely heard about LinkedIn, haven't you? It's the ultimate social network dedicated to professionals, and it's bursting with prospects for your career path ahead. With a massive community of over 900 million professionals from more than 200 countries, it's a pretty big playground! But as a high school or college student, you might be scratching your head and asking, "Why LinkedIn?" or "How do I even use it to link up?" No stress, we're here to unravel it all for you.

First order of business, you need a profile that really pops. This means a professional photo (remember to leave the beach snaps for Instagram), an attention-grabbing headline, and a summary that's all about showcasing you. Be sure to toss in your education, any work experiences, and the cool skills you're packing.

Here are some Linkedin best practices to keep you on top of your online networking game:

Personalize your connection invites: When you're reaching out to someone, always tag on a personal note. Share why you want to link up and how you stumbled across them. It proves you've taken a sec to learn about them and makes it way more likely they'll accept your request.

Stay on the ball: Aim to like, comment, and share posts from your connections. It keeps your relationships buzzing and helps you get noticed on the platform.

Sharing is winning: Share articles, news, and updates that align with what you're passionate about. It shows you're in the know and brings value to your network. If someone in your circle needs advice or a helping hand, jump in. It'll solidify your relationships and could open doors to awesome opportunities.

Join the squad: Get involved in LinkedIn groups that vibe with your interests. It's a fantastic way to connect with other pros and showcase your smarts.

Stay plugged in: Try to engage with your network daily, even if it's just for a few minutes. It'll keep you tuned in with industry news, trends, and opportunities.

Flaunt your know-how: Think about writing and sharing articles on LinkedIn. It can help position you as a guru in your field and draw more people with similar interests to your profile.

Keep branching out: Regularly scout for and link up with folks in your area of interest. The bigger your network gets, the more opportunities you'll uncover for teaming up.

If you stick with it and keep adding value to your LinkedIn network, you'll soon be on track to build a powerful online presence and create meaningful connections.

Mastering Career Fair Networking

Ever hit up a career fair? If you're in high school or college, these events are like your golden ticket to discovering potential careers, mingling with pros in the field, and building connections that could supercharge your future. But how can you squeeze every drop of goodness out of these events? How do you network like a superstar and leave a memorable impression? That's where we come in. We're here to prepare you for crushing it at your next career fair.

Finding career fairs – on the ground or online:

You can count on your school: Your school or college likely has a career center that's all about helping you guys find career fairs and other golden opportunities. Keep your eyes peeled for announcements, and newsletters, or drop by the career center to scoop the intel on upcoming events.

Surf the web: There are tons of sites like Eventbrite, Indeed, or Handshake that flag up career fairs in your local scene or even online. Sign up for their newsletters or create an account, and you'll get updates about what's going down soon. Plus, we've listed some more cool websites in the resources section.

Plug into professional associations: Some career realms have associations that whip up career fairs or networking events. Becoming a member could unlock doors to members-only events and opportunities. So go on, do a quick Google, and see what's cooking!

Careers Fair Etiquette

First things first, dress to impress. It doesn't mean you have to wear a three-piece suit or a ballgown, but putting on your best 'business casual' outfit will do the trick. And don't forget the magic accessory, a friendly smile! It's the perfect way to show you're approachable and positive.

Now, let's talk resumes. You're gonna want to have it ready for when you've just had a great chat with a potential employer, and they ask for your resume. So, come equipped with several copies of your well-polished resume. It's like your own little billboard advertising how awesome and professional you are!

Finally, we've got the elevator pitch. It's not as scary as it sounds, promise. It's just a quick and snappy introduction that showcases your talents, your experience, and what you're hoping to scoop up in a job or internship. Practicing it before the fair will help you sell your super skills with confidence.

Follow these best practices for your elevator pitch and it'll be hard for you to fail!

1. Keep it short: Make your pitch around 30-60 seconds long. Get straight to the point and highlight your best qualities.

2. Know your audience: Customize your pitch for each situation. Think about who you're talking to and what they might be interested in hearing.

3. Start strong: Begin with an attention-grabbing statement or question to hook the listener right away.

4. Highlight what makes you special: Talk about your unique skills, experiences, and what sets you apart from others.

5. Practice makes perfect: Rehearse your pitch multiple times to sound confident and natural. Get feedback from others and make improvements.

6. Show enthusiasm: Let your passion shine through your words and body language. Be excited about what you have to offer.

7. Be flexible: Adapt your pitch based on the situation and the person you're talking to.

8. Seek feedback: Ask for input from mentors or friends and make adjustments to make your pitch even better.

Remember, your elevator pitch is your chance to make a great first impression. With practice and confidence, you'll be able to showcase your talents and leave a lasting impact.

Tips to help you make the most of careers fairs

Step into the Employer's Shoes

Let's play pretend for a bit. Imagine you're the one manning a booth at a career fair. What would you be looking for in a student who rolls up to chat? It's a super important question to ask yourself. Usually, the people behind the booths are on the hunt for young folks who are truly keen on their company, have a decent idea about what they do, and can hold a good conversation. Wow them by doing your homework before the fair and come ready to ask clever, thought-provoking questions. Remember, they're there to spot potential future stars, and that could totally be you!

Navigating the Career Fair Jungle

Career fairs can feel like you've walked into a maze, right? So many booths, so little time! But chill, we've got some killer tips to help you navigate it. First up, get a game plan together. Work out which companies really float your boat and make a beeline for their booths first. But keep your eyes open for unexpected gems - you might find something awesome in the least expected place! If you're feeling a bit jittery, that's totally cool. Take a deep breath, pace yourself, and remember, everyone's there to mingle.

Business Cards: Your New BFFs

Business cards might feel a bit like last century, but trust us, they're still a big deal. When you meet someone cool at a career fair, ask for their business card. It's an easy way to remember who you chatted with and how to reach out to them later. Pro tip: after snagging their card, write a couple of quick notes on the back to jog your memory about your conversation. This can be super handy when you're following up later!

Conquering the Virtual Career Fair World

In this era of all things digital, virtual career fairs are becoming the norm. They're a touch different from the face-to-face ones, but no sweat, we've got your back. First off, treat it just like you would an in-person event – dress sharp and find a quiet, tidy spot for your background. Do a tech check before the event to make sure your internet and gear are all good to go.

And just like with physical fairs, come armed with well-researched questions and a snappy intro about yourself. Also, keep your eyes on the chat box, as that's where a lot of the crucial details pop up. Finally, don't forget to follow up. Fire off a LinkedIn connection request or an email to thank them for their time. It shows you're serious about the opportunities they're offering.

With these tricks up your sleeve, you'll be all set to slay any career fair - virtual or otherwise - and forge some super valuable connections. Remember, it's all about putting your best foot forward and showing that you're genuinely interested.

Uncovering Networking Goldmines: Other Places You Can Find Your Next Big Connection

Your Family and Buddies: Let your family and friends in on your career dreams and ask if they happen to know someone who's already in the industry you're eyeing. You never know, your Aunt Sally might have a friend who's a big-shot in the field you're interested in. Or your best friend's dad could have worked in that industry for years. So, don't be shy and ask around. You could land some cool introductions or insider info!

Part-time Jobs and Internships: Here's another hotspot for networking - your part-time job or internship. These places are filled with pros who've been in the game longer than you and can give you some solid career advice. So, make an effort to connect with your colleagues and bosses.

Online Hangouts: Have you checked out online forums, social media groups, or communities related to your career interests? These digital spaces are perfect for connecting with industry pros and fellow enthusiasts. Chime in on discussions, ask thoughtful questions and share your own insights. It's a great way to make connections from the comfort of your own home.

Workshops and Conferences: Keep an eye out for workshops, seminars, or conferences that revolve around your field of interest. Not only will you gain a ton of knowledge, but you'll also get to rub elbows with industry gurus, potential employers, and like-minded attendees. So, grab those opportunities and network away!

Professional Associations: Did you know there are organizations just for professionals in specific fields? Look for ones relevant to your career dreams. Many of them offer memberships for students, which can open doors to exclusive resources, events, and networking opportunities

By tapping into these networking goldmines, you'll grow your professional circle, putting you on the fast track to finding awesome mentors and opportunities in the career you're stoked about.

Alright, now that you've uncovered these networking goldmines and started mining those precious connections, what's next? Well, remember, it's not just about collecting contacts, it's about cultivating relationships, especially with mentors and role models who can provide invaluable guidance. So, in the next section, we're going to dig into how to build these rewarding relationships and tap into the power of mentorship.

Mentors and Role Models: The Power of Guidance and Support

Mentors and role models are the people you look up to, those who get you hyped about your future, and dish out seriously helpful advice to guide your career journey. They could be anyone from successful pros in your dream job, to your teachers, or even family members who are totally nailing it in their own careers. As you continue on your networking journey, you're bound to cross paths with these inspiring folks.

Here's why finding a mentor can supercharge your career journey

1. **They've got your back:** Mentors and role models serve up wisdom, guidance, and the kind of cheerleading that helps you tackle tough decisions and roadblocks like a boss.

2. **They're a living, breathing career guide:** Forget textbooks and online courses, mentors and role models offer real-life stories that are more gripping than any novel. They'll share their wins, their slip-ups, and the hard-learned lessons you won't find anywhere else.

3. **They're your ticket to more connections:** Your mentor or role model didn't get to where they are alone. They've got their own squad of connections and they can introduce you to some pretty awesome people. This means more chances to learn and grow.

4. **They're your confidence boosters:** When you have a mentor or role model who's rooting for you, it can turbocharge your confidence and drive you to chase your dreams.

That being said, finding the right mentor, and building a strong relationship with them, doesn't just happen overnight. It's a journey that requires time, patience, and the right moves.

Here's how to find and bond with potential mentors:

1. **Identify potential mentors:** This is your first step! Think about the people you admire in your chosen field. They could be successful professionals, teachers, or even family members who've aced their careers. Your dream mentor should be someone whose career journey inspires you and aligns with your own goals.

2. **Reach out thoughtfully:** Here's where your networking skills come into play. Drop them a message or an email expressing your admiration for their work and ask if they would be open to sharing some advice or insights. Or

better yet give them something valuable (the law of reciprocity is real!). Remember to be genuine and respectful, nobody likes a brown-noser!

3. **Keep it light initially:** Don't ask for mentorship right off the bat. Start by asking for guidance on a specific issue, or request a brief meeting to discuss their experiences. It's about laying the groundwork for a potential mentoring relationship.

4. **Nurture the relationship:** If they agree to help, great! Now, it's about building rapport and trust. Consistent communication is key, but be mindful of their time. Ask for advice, share your progress, and always show gratitude for their support.

5. **Officially ask for mentorship:** After you've developed a good rapport, you can consider popping the question. Remember to clarify what you're hoping to get from the mentorship and assure them that you're committed to learning and growing.

Now, let's talk about what you can do to make this relationship a two-way street and keep your mentors interested in sharing their golden nuggets of wisdom with you. After all, mentorship isn't a one-sided deal.

1. **Show progress and initiative:** There's no better way to show your gratitude than by taking their advice seriously. Show them you're making progress and you're dedicated to your growth.

2. **Offer your help:** While you may not be able to offer professional guidance, there are other ways to add value. Maybe your mentor needs a fresh perspective, or help with something you're good at. Don't hesitate to offer your assistance.

3. **Keep them in the loop:** Sharing updates, asking for advice, and maintaining regular communication will show your mentor that you appreciate their

support.

As you journey through your career, your mentors and role models will act as your navigators, helping you steer through challenges and make the most of opportunities. Remember, the key to a successful mentorship is mutual respect, open communication, and an eagerness to learn.

But you might be wondering how to tap into all that valuable insight. Well, one super effective method is through informational interviews.

Informational Interviews

Informational interviews are basically casual conversations with someone who's got their game on in a job or industry you're interested in. These one-on-one chats are your golden ticket to insider knowledge about a specific career, the vibe of a workplace, or what makes a company tick. Don't mix it up with job interviews, though. These are all about quenching your curiosity, asking all the questions you want, and making cool new connections.

So why should you care about informational interviews?

Here's the deal! They're an amazing way for you to explore different career paths and fine-tune what your dream job looks like. You get to pull back the curtain and discover the real-deal day-to-day of a specific job or industry (No more wondering, "What does a data analyst actually do all day?").

Plus, you get insider tips and advice straight from the pros, which can totally help you shine if you choose to dive into that field. But that's not all! These chats also let you create awesome connections with industry pros who might become your mentors, your cheerleaders, or even your future colleagues (How cool is that?). And as if all of that wasn't enough, by making a memorable impression, you could be unlocking doors to future job offers.

How to find informational interviews?

1. **Leverage your network:** Reach out to family, friends, teachers, or mentors, and ask if they know anyone working in your area of interest.
2. **Use LinkedIn:** Search for professionals in your desired field, and send them a personalized message requesting a brief informational interview
3. **Attend networking events:** Introduce yourself to professionals at career fairs, conferences, or workshops, and ask if you can follow up with an informational interview.

Questions to ask during an informational interview:

1. What does a typical day look like for you in your role?
2. How did you get started in this field? What was your career journey like?
3. What skills or experiences do you think are essential for success in this role or industry?
4. What do you enjoy most about your job? What are the biggest challenges you face?
5. Can you recommend any resources (books, websites, organizations) for someone interested in this field?
6. What advice do you have for someone just starting out in this industry?

Just remember, these informational interviews are your golden ticket to widening your network and getting priceless insights about your future career. Go into them with a curious mind, be mindful of their time, and don't forget to send a thank-you note after!

Once you've made these connections, it's all about keeping that relationship alive and kicking. After all, a solid network is all about mutual respect, helping each other out, and regular chit-chat.

Keeping Professional Relationships Alive & Kicking

So, you've put in the hard yards and scored some awesome connections – high five to you! But remember, it's one thing to collect Pokemon cards, but it's another thing to keep them safe and shiny, right? The same goes for your professional relationships. These connections can become even more valuable over time, just like that holographic Charizard!

Now let's talk about how to keep these relationships alive and kicking. Staying in touch can be as easy as sending a quick email, text, or LinkedIn message every now and then. A "Congrats!" on a promotion or sharing a neat article you read can do wonders. And always be ready to lend a hand, whether that's sharing job leads, introducing them to other cool people, or giving helpful feedback.

Next up, don't forget about networking events and conferences – they're your front-row ticket to catching up with contacts, staying visible, and keeping up with what's hot in your industry. And hey, if your contacts have a win, be their number-one fan! A quick message of congrats, a social media shoutout, or sharing their good news can really strengthen your bond.

Remember, it's all about being real. Authenticity is the key to trust and long-lasting relationships. And don't let life's whirlwind let you forget your network – setting calendar reminders to check in with your contacts can keep those lines of communication buzzing.

By putting these relationships near the top of your priorities list, you're creating a powerhouse network that'll seriously boost your long-term career game. Trust, mutual support, and genuine connections are the building blocks of the strongest relationships.

And... that's a wrap on our networking chapter! Remember, making friends in your career field is a journey, not a destination. With all the tips and tricks we've chatted about, you're ready to start making some epic connections and bringing your career dreams to life.

In the next chapter, we'll dive into the exciting realm of real-world experience, where you'll learn how to gain hands-on knowledge and make a splash in your chosen field.

Chapter 10 - There's No Substitute for Real-World Experience

"The best way to predict the future is to create it." - Peter Drucker

So, you've been at school for years, right? You've smashed algebra, aced your language arts projects, and maybe even scored big at a few science fairs. But there's a whole wide world beyond those classroom doors that's super excited to meet you. That's where the magic of real-world work experience steps in!

Ever played a video game where your character levels up by tackling challenges and stacking up xp? Real-world work experience is kinda like that for your life. Every task you tick off, every problem you solve, and every new face you meet can help you score experience points in the game of life. You'll acquire new skills, learn how to handle a variety of situations, and get the 411 on how all those things you've been studying at school apply in the real world. It's like turbocharging your education!

Snagging real-world experience is how you buff up your resume. Think of your resume as your personal 'best of' montage. It flaunts your skills, experiences, and achievements to potential employers. Having real-world work experience to slot into your resume is like sprinkling in some epic action sequences into that montage. It signals to employers, "Hey, I've been out there in the world, getting stuff done. I've got the chops to be an MVP on your team!" It helps your resume shine and shows that you're serious about your career journey.

Ever taken a risk and tried a new ice cream flavor, only to stumble upon a new favorite? Just like that, stepping into the real world can give you a taste of jobs you might end up totally vibing with! Maybe you thought you wanted to be a graphic designer, but then you intern at a marketing agency and realize project management is your jam. Or perhaps you clock in some part-time hours at a vet clinic and discover you're crazy about animal care. Real-world experiences can help you figure out what you love doing, what you're an ace at, and what you want to chase in the future.

So, as you can see, real-world work experience is like a power-up for your career. It adds to your education, upgrades your resume, and helps you uncover your passions. It's a crucial pitstop on your journey, so let's dive into more ways to score this experience in the upcoming sections!

The Value of Part-time Jobs

Imagine earning cash, leveling up your skills, learning the money game, and making new connections, all at the same time. That's the magic of a part-time job!

Maybe you're flipping burgers, restocking shelves, or tutoring kiddos – whatever it is, you're gathering an arsenal of skills. Stuff like time management, communication, and customer service. Basically, each task you tackle carves out your unique skills map.

Now, let's talk about the moolah. It's no secret that one of the major perks of a part-time job is the cash you get to pocket. Saving for the latest gaming console, eyeing that concert ticket, or just starting to stash some money for college, there's something pretty sweet about earning your own dough. But the real deal? Learning the ropes of money management. Budgeting, saving, and maybe even a touch of investing – it's like taking a crash course on adulting.

And don't forget about all the networking opportunities that come with it. Part-time jobs are the perfect platform to put that into action. Your co-workers, managers, and even the customers you help can be the seeds of your future networking tree. Who knows, the person you helped find the perfect product last week could be the key to your dream job tomorrow!

In short, part-time jobs are not just about pocketing extra change (although, let's be honest, that's a pretty cool part). They're your ticket to skill-building, money mastery, and networking nirvana. Talk about a career hat trick!

The Role of Volunteer Work

Ever thought about volunteering? It's not just about giving back to your community (although that's super important!). It's also a golden chance to develop skills you wouldn't get from a job and make your resume shine. Let's dig into this a bit more:

Volunteering is like a secret training ground for soft skills. You know, those skills that can't be measured by a test but are super important in life? Stuff like teamwork, leadership, problem-solving, and empathy. Whether you're organizing a charity event, helping out at the local food bank, or tutoring younger kids, you're picking up these valuable skills. Plus, they'll help you in any career you choose, promise!

159

There's also something really special about knowing that your actions are making a positive impact. Volunteering lets you be a superhero in your own community, helping those who need it most. It's not just about what you give; it's also about what you get in return - a sense of fulfillment and purpose.

Let's face it, colleges and employers love seeing volunteer work on a resume. It sets you apart from the crowd and shows that you're dedicated, compassionate, and willing to go the extra mile. It's like saying, "Hey, I'm not just awesome at what I do; I also care about making the world a better place."

So, volunteering? It's a win-win-win. You develop crucial skills, make a difference, and boost your resume. Now that's what we call a power move! Coming up next, we're going to talk about two more ways to gain real-world experience.

Job Shadowing and Internships

Let's dive into a couple more ways to sample the working world: job shadowing and internships. Consider these as your exclusive trailers for what your future career might be like.

Picture job shadowing as being a career spy for a day. You get to tag along with a pro on their job and witness what they do on the regular. It's like scoring a VIP pass to a concert, but instead of tunes, you're scoring insights on a particular job. It's an amazing way to explore different careers without signing a long-term contract. Plus, you get to fire away all the questions you've got!

Internships, on the flip side, are kinda like dipping your toes into the career path you're seeking. They're short-term gigs that arm you with industry-specific experience. Some come with a paycheck, some don't (yeah, we get it, that bit can be a letdown). But the real prize? The hands-on experience and the contacts you'll make in the field you're into. Consider it a trial run for a career path you might be eyeing.

Now, you might be thinking, "This sounds awesome, but where do I even start looking for these opportunities?" Top question! Kick things off by having a chat with your school counselor and don't overlook job search websites and even LinkedIn. And your network can be super handy here too. Maybe your cousin's friend's mom works in an area you're curious about. Don't be shy, ask around!

As you keep amassing real-world experience and exploring diverse career trails, you might bump into the thrilling world of freelancing, where your skills and talents can sparkle in a flexible and independent way.

Chapter 11 - The Amazing World of Freelancing

"Do what you love, and you'll never work another day in your life." - *Confucius*

Once upon a time, I bumped into this super rad thing called freelancing. No joke, you get to work on your own terms, pick the projects you vibe with, and run your own time. Sounded like a dream gig, especially for someone like me, always on the lookout for the freedom to blaze my own trail. If you're also hunting for that kind of freedom and flexibility, then freelancing might just be the journey you've been waiting to embark on!

Freelancing is all about working independently, and serving your skills and services to clients on a project-by-project basis, rather than being a full-time worker bee for a single hive. The freelancing universe is jam-packed with mind-blowing opportunities, from writing and graphic design to web development and social media wizardry, and so much more. It's like a treasure trove of chances waiting for you to dive in!

You're probably wondering, "But I'm just a teen! Can I really pull this off?" The answer is a resounding, "Yes!" You're never too young to start sharpening your skills and carving out your own niche. In fact, freelancing can be a great way for you to gain experience, craft a portfolio, and make some extra dough, all while juggling your school responsibilities. Sounds like a win-win, right?

In this chapter, we're going to deep-dive into the freelancing scene for teens, from crafting a jaw-dropping portfolio to netting your first clients.

Building a Freelance Portfolio

Think of a freelance portfolio as your showcase, putting your skills, epic talents, and shiny achievements on display. It's super important because it lets potential clients peep into your skillset and helps them figure out if you're the right fit for their mission. Put simply, it's your key to unlocking the freelance kingdom, especially for teens who may not have loads of work experience just yet.

Here are some steps for building an awesome freelance portfolio, even if you're fresh to the scene:

Unleash your creative superpower: Reflect on the kind of work you're excited to show off. Are you a wordsmith, a design whiz, a code ninja, or perhaps a social media maestro? Whatever your talent, concentrate on crafting a few standout pieces that spotlight your abilities.

Give props to school projects: Don't underestimate the projects you've undertaken as part of school commitments, they can totally feature in your portfolio. That killer essay or art project you aced? Toss it into your portfolio!

Plunge into personal projects: Engaging in passion projects can help you learn, evolve, and produce cool stuff for your portfolio. Launch a blog, design a logo, or pen a short story – your imagination's the limit!

Lend your services for free (just to kick things off): Think about doing a few mini-projects for buddies, family, or local groups to gain experience and beef up your portfolio. But hey, once you've got a rockin' portfolio, it's high time to start getting paid!

Brag about your wins: Awards, publications, or other awesome acknowledgments deserve a spot in your portfolio. Show potential clients you're a shooting star!

Amp up the visual appeal: A striking, tidy portfolio can do wonders. Use online platforms like Behance or Wix to whip up a slick, professional-looking portfolio that's a breeze to explore and share.

Keep it fresh: Spruce up your portfolio as you rack up experience and master new skills. You're an ever-evolving freelancer, and your portfolio should narrate that adventure!

With a bit of grit, a splash of creativity, and some hard graft, you'll soon have a freelance portfolio that leaves clients gobsmacked and stoked to collaborate with you.

Landing Freelance Gigs

Hunting for freelance work can feel like an impossible task (especially as you're starting out), but don't sweat it – we're here to guide you! Let's check out how to find those freelance gigs that'll jazz up your life (and beef up your wallet!)

Sound the trumpets: Announce to your pals, family, and anyone who'll lend an ear that you're venturing into freelancing. You never know who might need your talents or knows someone who does. Trust me, word of mouth is like a magic spell, and it's a fabulous way to get your first clients.

Get social media savvy: Jazz up your profiles to include your freelance offerings and broadcast your work to the world. Platforms like LinkedIn, Twitter, and Instagram are your stages to connect with potential clients, network with fellow freelancers, and make your name sparkle.

Dive into online freelance hubs: Websites like Upwork, Fiverr, and Freelancer are like treasure islands brimming with freelance gigs. Set up a profile, scour for gigs, and apply for projects that match your skill set. Bear in mind, competition can be tough, so ensure your pitches are absolute fire! Peek at a comprehensive list of freelance hubs in the resources section.

Hang where the clients do: Niche job boards, forums, and online communities can be a jackpot for freelance work. Sniff out spots where your ideal clients chill and start forging connections.

Network like a rockstar: Networking can be a total game changer when on the hunt for freelance gigs. Hit up local meetups, workshops, and events tied to your industry, and don't be shy about introducing yourself and swapping contact details. You never know where a random chat might lead!

Fire off some hot cold emails: The term "cold email" refers to reaching out to potential clients or contacts with no prior introduction or connection, meaning the recipient is in the dark about who you are. Do some detective work on companies or individuals you'd kill to work with and drop them a personalized email presenting yourself and your offerings. Show them how you can amp up their business and simplify their lives. As cold emails pop up uninvited, it's crucial to make a positive and memorable impact to up your chances of bagging a response.

Stay alert: Sometimes, freelance opportunities pop up where you least expect them. Scan local newspapers, bulletin boards, and community websites for job ads or businesses that could do with your skills.

Remember, finding freelance work is like riding a roller coaster. Sometimes, it's all butterflies and high-fives, and other times, it can be a bit of a headache. But as long as you keep hustling, continue honing your skills, and never throw in the towel, you'll navigate through the maze and onto the road to freelance triumph. So get out there, chase those dreams, and morph your passion into a booming freelance career!

Setting Rates and Negotiating Contracts

Ever stood in front of the snack aisle, torn between the cheaper snack or the slightly pricier but super yummy one? That's kind of what deciding your freelance rates and hammering out contracts can feel like. You want to hit that sweet spot where you're getting paid your worth without making clients run for the hills. But hey, no worries, here are some handy tips to help you decide on your rates and negotiate like a boss.

First things first, you've got to figure out what your skills and experience are worth out there in the big wide world. Check out what the going rate in your field is, and think about stuff like your skill level, how complex the project is, and what the client's budget looks like.

There are a bunch of ways to charge for your freelancing magic – by the hour, per project, or even a retainer fee. Think about what makes the most sense for you and your clients. Just remember, if you're charging by the hour, keep an eagle eye on the clock.

When talking about rates with clients, stand tall and be assertive. Remember, you're a skilled pro offering killer services, so don't sell yourself short. It's okay to haggle a bit, but know your worth, and don't be scared to stick to your guns.

A solid contract is your biggest ally in the freelance world. It lays out what work you'll be doing when it's due, how you'll get paid, and other key details, so everyone knows what's up. There are heaps of online resources to help you whip up a custom contract that's got all the bases covered.

Be prepared to be a bit flexible. Sometimes, getting to an agreement means a bit of give and take. Be open to tweaking your rates or offering a few extra services to land a deal that works for you and the client. Just remember not to give away too much – you deserve to get paid fairly for your work.

Once you've agreed on the details, make sure to get it all in writing. A signed contract is your safety net if any disagreements pop up later, so hold off on starting any work until you've got one in hand.

Remember to stay on top of your game and keep an eye on all your invoices and payments. Be sure to send out invoices on time and chase up any late payments. And don't forget to put some money aside for taxes – freelancing means you've got to handle your own tax stuff. I could dive deep into this topic, but I won't bore you with details that tax experts can give you.

Remember, deciding your rates and nailing contracts can feel like walking a tightrope, but with a bit of research, confidence, and flexibility, you'll be on your way to a freelancing career that's not just rewarding creatively but also fills up your piggy bank.

Freelancing 101: The Legal and Money Stuff Made Simple

So, you're ready to plunge into the freelancing sea, which also means it's time to wrap your head around the legal and cash part of your biz. As a freelancer, getting a grip on this stuff is uber important to keep things sailing smoothly and sidestep any hiccups down the line. Here are some key areas you should zone in on:

1. **Taxes:** As a freelancer, you're the captain of your tax ship. This could include income tax, self-employment tax, and other taxes depending on where you drop anchor. Keep a log of all your earnings and expenses, and don't hesitate to ask a tax guru for a helping hand with all the tax stuff.

2. **Contracts:** Drafting and negotiating contracts with clients is crucial to safeguard your interests and spell out the work, payment terms, and other important details. A sturdy contract can prevent mix-ups and lend you a legal backup if any snags pop up. If contracts make your head spin, consider nabbing some legal advice or tap into online contract templates to set sail.

3. **Invoicing and payment tracking:** Get a system going for billing clients and keeping tabs on payments. This includes setting payment terms, like due dates and late fees, and maintaining a record of all transactions. A solid invoicing and payment tracking system can help you monitor your cash flow and ensure you're getting paid promptly for your hard work.

4. **Insurance:** Depending on the kind of freelancing you're into, you might need to consider insurance to shield yourself from any potential risks. Dive into what types of insurance relate to your field and find out what coverage suits your needs best.

5. **Business structure:** Based on where you're located and the size of your freelancing gig, you might need to establish a formal business structure,

like a sole proprietorship, limited liability company (LLC), or a corporation. Each comes with its own set of legal and tax puzzles, so it's vital to do your homework and figure out which option fits you like a glove.

By mastering the legal and financial side of freelancing, you'll be better equipped to steer your business and concentrate on expanding your career as a self-reliant whizz. And remember, this stuff might seem like a brain-twister at first, but with time it becomes like second nature.

So there it is! Armed with determination, elbow grease, and the right tools in your arsenal, the sky's the limit. So go out there and rock it, teen freelancers! Next we're going to take a look at what it takes to start your own business and start out on your entrepreneurial journey.

Chapter 12 - Introduction to Entrepreneurship: Starting Your Own Venture

"The entrepreneur always searches for change, responds to it, and exploits it as an opportunity." – Peter Drucker

Alright, you've definitely bumped into the term "entrepreneurship" before, right? But what's it all about? As an entrepreneur, you kickstart your own business and you've got the reins of everything that's going on (well, at least in the beginning!). From cooking up a crazy-cool idea to finding folks who dig what you're offering, you call the shots.

And let's make one thing crystal clear, we're not just talking about garage sales or lemonade stands here (although, those are totally valid first steps!). Entrepreneurs can fire up all sorts of ventures, like designing a slick app, launching a trendy fashion brand, whipping up tasty treats in a cafe, or even starting a space exploration outfit (Elon Musk, we're looking at you!).

But being an entrepreneur isn't all about selling stuff. It's a chance to flex your creative muscles, solve pesky problems, and even make a splash in the world. It's about spotting a need or a hiccup and thinking, "Hey, I can sort that out!" And then, you know, actually getting out there and doing the darn thing.

Entrepreneurship as a career path? Absolutely, it's a legit choice! You're your own boss, you set your own timetable, and you chase after what lights you up. Plus, there's no ceiling to what you can accomplish. If your biz takes flight, you could leave a serious mark, rake in the big bucks, and maybe even snag a spot in the limelight!

But hey, remember, rocking the entrepreneur life is like riding a wild roller coaster. There are thrilling highs, challenging lows, unexpected twists and turns, and occasionally, you might feel a tad topsy-turvy. But if you're game for the thrill, entrepreneurship could be your golden ticket to an unforgettable journey.

The Ups and Downs of Entrepreneurship: The Cool Perks and Real Challenges

Alright, let's get real about entrepreneurship. It's not all sunshine and rainbows, but it's not all stormy skies either. It's kind of like a rollercoaster ride with some amazing highs and a few scary dips. Let's take a look at the rewards and tricky challenges of being your own boss.

The Pros

You Get to Be Your Own Boss: You call the shots. Want to work in your pajamas? Cool. Feel like taking a midday break for a quick game session? Go for it. You get to make the rules.

Follow Your Passion: You're not stuck doing something you don't love. You can turn your favorite hobby, your passion, or that crazy cool idea you had in the shower, into your job.

In the beginning, you might need to do some jobs for your business that you aren't a big fan of. But hey, as your business grows, you'll have the chance to pass on these tasks to folks who are ace at them and totally dig them!

Unlimited Potential: There's no cap on how much you can earn or how big your business can grow. If your idea is a hit, you could end up being the next big thing. (Ever heard of a guy named Mark Zuckerberg?)

Make a Difference: Entrepreneurs solve problems and meet needs. You have the chance to create something that can really help people and make the world a better place.

The Cons

It Can Be Time-Consuming: Starting a business can take a ton of time. Late nights, early mornings, and weekends might become your new normal. Although if you work extremely hard and give in a couple hours extra after work or school they really do add up. Consistency is key!

Money Matters: Businesses need money to start and keep running. You might need to save up, find investors, or take some financial risks.

Stress Alert: With great power comes great stress. Deciding everything, dealing with problems, and feeling responsible for other people (like employees or customers) can be a lot to handle.

Failure is a Thing: Not every business is a hit. Some entrepreneurs have to try a few (or a lot of) times before they strike gold. Failure can be tough, but it's also a great teacher.

So, there you have it, the real deal about entrepreneurship. It's exciting, rewarding, challenging, and sometimes a little scary. But if you're the kind of person who loves a good adventure and has the right skills, it just might be the perfect ride for you!

Essential Skills for Entrepreneurs: Creativity, Resilience, Leadership, and Adaptability

Remember way back in chapter 1 where we discussed essential skills and traits that you'd need to cultivate as you navigate this career path you have chosen? It's no different from being an entrepreneur. When you're an entrepreneur and a leader of a team, you need to possess some key skills to drive your project forward in good times and bad.

Creativity: The Master of Innovation

Entrepreneurs need to break out of the norm, craft unique ideas, and spot fresh solutions to issues. If you're the kind of person who's always sketching crazy contraptions in your notebook or daydreaming about the next cool trend, you've got this skill on lockdown!

Resilience: The Bounce-Back Whizz

Life in the business lane doesn't always run smooth. Sometimes, you might hit a speed bump or even crash. But hey, even superheroes have off days, right? The important thing is to dust yourself off and keep going. Resilience is all about bouncing back from tough times, learning from the low moments, and never letting a hiccup hold you back.

Leadership: The Squad Leader

Just like a superhero rallying their team, entrepreneurs often need to steer the ship. Whether you're motivating a team, convincing investors, or winning over your customers, stepping up as a great leader is indispensable.

Adaptability: The Quick-Change Artist

The business world can be a wild ride. One moment you're cruising, and the next, you're dealing with an unexpected twist. This is where your adaptability super skill shines. Being able to switch up your plans, tweak your ideas, or change your game plan on the spot is a key part of entrepreneurial life.

Just remember, like any skill, these ones can take time and practice to perfect. But don't sweat it, each challenge is just another opportunity to level up.

Your First Steps to Business Stardom: The Startup Adventure Begins

So, you've decided to start your own business? That's awesome! But wait, where do you even begin? It's like planning a journey to a new city. You need a map, some planning, and a sense of adventure! Let's break it down into the first basic steps.

Step 1: Dream up Your Business Idea: The 'Aha!' Moment

Think about something you're passionate about or a problem you want to solve. Your business idea can spring from there. It's like that lightbulb moment in cartoons. Ding! You've got an idea!

Step 2: Market Research: Detective Mode On

Now, you need to play detective. Find out who else is doing what you want to do. This is your competition. What are they doing right? What could you do better? And, most importantly, who are your customers going to be? What do they want or need? Gathering this info is called market research.

Step 3: Business Planning: Drawing the Treasure Map

Here's where you draw the map to your treasure, also known as a business plan. This is a document that outlines what your business will do, how it will operate, who your customers are, and how you plan to make money. It's like your game plan, your secret sauce recipe.

Remember, starting your own business is an adventure, and every adventure needs a bit of planning. But don't worry if you're feeling a bit overwhelmed. Every big journey starts with a single step. So, take a deep breath, put on your entrepreneurial adventurer's hat, and let's get started!

Alright, you've now got the lowdown on entrepreneurship—the cool bits, the tricky parts, the superpowers you need, and the first leaps to make if you're keen to jump in, plus some insanely useful resources. Next up, we're going to tackle something crucial in your career journey—balancing work and school.

Chapter 13 - Mastering the Balancing Act: Juggling Work and School

"Life is like riding a bicycle. To keep your balance, you must keep moving."

- Albert Einstein

I f you've been following along, by now you've probably got a solid handle on all the ways you can jumpstart your career. From part-time jobs and internships to freelancing and even starting your own venture—there's a world of exciting opportunities out there. But here's the tricky part: how do you manage all this work stuff without flunking geometry or missing out on fun times with your friends?

Juggling school work, job responsibilities, extracurricular activities, and (let's not forget) your well-deserved leisure time can feel like you're a plate spinner in a circus. But don't worry, we've got your back! In this chapter, we'll navigate through strategies and tips that'll help you keep all those plates in the air.

Remember, every superhero needs a sidekick, and in this chapter, you'll find yours. From time management hacks and prioritizing pointers to tips on maintaining your health and well-being, this chapter is chock-full of wisdom to help you manage your dual roles as a student and a working professional.

So, strap in as we embark on this journey of mastering the art of balance. Together, we'll ensure you can ace that test, crush your job responsibilities, and still find time to chill with your friends, or just binge-watch your favorite Netflix show.

The Challenge: Balancing School with Different Types of Work

So you've got school and work to juggle. Maybe that's a part-time job, an internship, some freelance hustle, or even your own startup. Sounds like you're trying to skateboard while flipping pancakes, right? Yeah, it's a bit of a wild ride. But guess what? With some practice and a few game-changing tips, you've totally got this.

Every type of work gig has its unique bumps. Maybe your part-time job clashes with your homework hours. Or your internship involves travel, making it tricky to hit those after-school activities. Freelancing? That's all on you, champ! You're the boss (pretty cool, huh?), but it also means you're the one ensuring you're hitting deadlines while also acing your tests. If you're running your own business, things might be even more of a rollercoaster because you've got to juggle... well, pretty much everything, from creating products to making sales to marketing.

Now, you're probably thinking, "That's a mountain to climb, how am I supposed to handle all that and still have time to binge-watch the latest season of my favorite series?" No worries, my friend! We're about to break it all down and equip you with the tools you need to not just hang on but totally rock this balancing act.

Remember, this is all about working smart, not just hard. So, stay with me, and by the end of this chapter, you'll be juggling those tasks like a total pro!

Time Management Strategies for Working Students

Prioritize So You Know What's Worth Doing Right Now!

Not every task is created equal. Yes, you read that right. Some tasks are urgent, some are important, and some are both. Urgent tasks are the ones demanding immediate attention. They're the tasks with the most immediate deadlines, like the paper due tomorrow or the shift you're scheduled to work tonight.

On the other hand, important tasks might not be shouting for your attention right now but have a significant impact on your long-term goals. Consider studying for your end-of-term exams or gaining extra responsibilities at work to boost your promotion chances.

So, how do you navigate this maze? One approach is by using the Eisenhower Box, a simple yet effective tool named after the 34th U.S. President, Dwight D. Eisenhower. It's so powerful even the busiest man on earth Elon Musk admits to using it!

The Eisenhower Box consists of four sections:

1. Urgent and Important (Do these tasks ASAP)

2. Not Urgent but Important (Plan to do these tasks)

3. Urgent but Not Important (Delegate these tasks if possible)

4. Not Urgent and Not Important (Do these tasks later)

Here's what an Eisenhower Box looks like:

Eisenhower Matrix

Using this tool, you can quickly figure out which tasks need your attention first. For example, you might have to balance studying for an exam (important, but not urgent) with writing a paper due tomorrow (urgent and important), and your friend is pleading with you to cover their work shift tonight (urgent, but not important). The Eisenhower Box helps you decide where your focus should be.

Remember, it's crucial, to be honest with yourself. It's easy to pretend that everything is both urgent and important, but that's a surefire ticket to feeling overwhelmed and burnt out. Let's focus our energies where they truly matter and let the rest wait their turn.

Effective Scheduling - The Key to Getting More Done Than You Possibly Knew You Could

Imagine your time as a big, empty box. How would you fill it? You've got smaller boxes labeled "School," "Work," "Homework," "Chill," and some others. Now, effective scheduling is like a high-stakes game of Tetris, where you need to place these boxes in the most efficient way, so you can manage all your roles without letting any box overflow.

First things first: To become a scheduling pro, you need to have a clear picture of what needs to be done and when. That means setting aside designated time blocks for each activity - school, work, study, and yes, even your Netflix or gaming time (We're humans, not robots, after all!).

Let's look at a day in the life of Sam, a part-time worker, and full-time student. Sam starts by blocking out time for school and work as these are non-negotiable. Next, Sam schedules homework time and some good old revision (you know, so they're not pulling an all-nighter before the big exam). And, of course, Sam reserves time for fun, relaxation, and self-care – because mental health matters, folks.

But how do you keep track of all this? The market is bursting with tools and techniques to make your scheduling journey a breeze. Here are a few options to consider:

1. **Digital Calendars:** Google Calendar, Outlook, Apple Calendar – you name it! These handy tools can send you reminders so you won't miss anything important.

2. **Productivity Apps:** Apps like Trello, Asana, or Todoist can help manage tasks, set deadlines, and even share your to-do list with a team (for those dreaded group projects).

3. Classic Pen-and-Paper Planners: There's something satisfying about crossing off tasks in a physical planner. Plus, studies suggest writing things down can help you remember them better.

Remember, it's not just about squeezing every minute of the day. It's about creating a schedule that allows you to juggle your responsibilities without dropping the ball on your personal well-being.

Beating Procrastination - Winning the Battle Against the Time Thieves

Okay, we need to talk about the big "P" – Procrastination. It's that annoying little voice in your head saying, "Hey, let's check Instagram… just for a minute," when you're neck-deep in Algebra homework. Or it might be the impulse to start a 10-hour gaming marathon just when that history essay is due. Procrastination can be the kryptonite to your super-productivity powers. So, how do you beat it?

Here are some tested and proven ways to knock procrastination out of the park:

1. **Break It Down**: You know that giant, terrifying task you've been avoiding? Break it down into smaller, less scary parts. Imagine having to clean your super-messy room (shudders). Instead of looking at it as one monumental task, break it down: first, tidy up your desk, then sort out the closet, next, deal with the pile of laundry, and so on. Small wins lead to big victories!

2. **The Pomodoro Technique**: Named after a tomato-shaped kitchen timer (yes, seriously!), this technique involves working for 25 minutes straight, then taking a 5-minute break. Repeat this cycle four times, and then take a longer break (say, 15-30 minutes). It's like mini sprints for your brain,

keeping it focused and fresh.

3. **Set Concrete Goals and Deadlines**: Saying, "I'll study Chemistry sometime this week," is like setting a trap for Procrastination to sneak in. Instead, make your goals specific and time-bound. "I'll study two chapters of Chemistry on Tuesday, from 4 PM to 6 PM," sounds way more commitment-like, doesn't it? SMART goals, remember?

Keep in mind, overcoming procrastination isn't about being perfect. It's about making progress. There might be days when the call of the procrastination sirens is too strong, and that's okay. Just pick yourself up, dust off those Dorito crumbs, and get back to the task. You've got this!

Clock In, Rock Out: Finding Your Productivity Power Hour!

Time for some fun biology! You know those natural rhythms your body follows, like getting hungry at certain times, or feeling sleepy at others? They're called circadian rhythms, and they're like your body's internal clock. What's super cool is that these rhythms also influence when we're most alert and focused. This is known as your "peak productivity time" or your "prime time." It's when your brain is ready to rock 'n' roll and handle those trickier tasks.

The tricky part? Everyone's prime time is different. Some folks are night owls, hitting their stride when the moon is high. Others are early birds, ready to conquer the world with the sunrise. Then, there are those who hit their productivity peak in the middle of the day. And guess what? There's no right or wrong time – it's all about figuring out what works best for you.

So, how do you find your prime time? You might already have a hunch. If you find that you always get your best studying done in the quiet hours of the morning, then you might be an early bird. On the other hand, if you find that you do your best work when everyone else has called it a day, then you might be a night owl.

But if you're not sure, try this for a week: Note down the times when you feel most alert and focused, and when you feel most sluggish. Then, look for patterns. You'll likely see certain times popping up again and again. Bingo, you've found your prime time!

Once you know your prime time, schedule your most challenging tasks for those hours. Have a difficult assignment? Tackle it during your prime time. Studying for a big test? Do your most intense study sessions when you're in your prime time. You'll be amazed at how much more you can get done when you're working with your body's natural rhythms, not against them.

Remember, it's not about squeezing work into every moment of your prime time. Breaks are essential, and it's okay if your prime time doesn't align perfectly with your school or work schedule. The key is making the most of those golden hours when you can. Now go find your prime time and show your tasks who's boss!

Juggling 101: Acing the Work-Study Balance Beam

So you've bagged a job (you rockstar, you!) but now you're wondering how to keep all these balls in the air. Fear not, my friend! We've got some tried-and-tested strategies to help you nail this juggling act.

Be a Negotiation Ninja

First things first, let's chat about your work hours. If you're working part-time, it's crucial that your schedule fits around your school commitments.

That might mean having a conversation with your boss about when you're available. Before you start hyperventilating at the thought, remember: communication is key, and most employers respect their employees who are also students. So, take a deep breath, wear your most confident smile, and discuss your need for flexible hours. Just remember to be honest, upfront, and considerate of the business needs too.

Goal-setting Goals

Next up, let's talk about setting realistic study goals. Look, we've all been there – promising ourselves we'll read five chapters, write two essays, and learn an entire semester's worth of equations in one afternoon. Yeah, right! Instead of setting yourself up for failure (and a load of stress), break your study load into manageable chunks. How about reading one chapter per day? Or writing a page of that essay every couple of hours? It's all about baby steps that lead to giant strides!

It's Okay to Say No

This one's tough, but oh-so-important: learning to say no. Listen, we get it. The extra cash from picking up an additional shift can be tempting, especially if you're saving up for something special. But when it's exam season or you're swimming in assignments, you need to prioritize. Remember, it's perfectly okay to say no to extra shifts, or to anything else that's going to put too much on your plate. Your future self, preparing for an exam without feeling completely overwhelmed, will thank you.

Keep these tips in your back pocket, and you'll find that the work-study balancing act isn't a terrifying tightrope walk – it's more like a well-choreographed dance. It might take a bit of practice to get the steps right, but once you do, you'll be twirling through your tasks with ease!

You're Not Alone: Don't Forget Self-Care and Getting Support When You Need It

Navigating the work-school highway is a bit like being a superhero. You've got a secret identity (your professional life) and your regular life (school). But even superheroes need to take a breather and tap into their support network sometimes. This is where self-care and seeking help come in!

Don't Forget to Breathe: Self-Care Essentials

You've heard the term 'self-care', right? Well, it's not just a fancy term for bubble baths and face masks (although those can be part of it!). It's about taking care of your physical and mental health. You see, your brain is kind of like a high-performance sports car - it runs best when it's well taken care of.

Ever tried studying after pulling an all-nighter? Or working a long shift without a break? Yeah, not fun. Taking breaks, getting enough sleep, eating healthily, and doing some physical activity are all crucial for staying in tip-top shape. You're not being lazy by taking care of yourself - you're being smart! And hey, it's scientifically proven that taking care of yourself boosts your performance both at work and school. So yeah, self-care? It's a big deal.

Rally Your Team: The Power of Support

As much as we'd all like to think we're indestructible superheroes, sometimes even Batman needs Robin. When the going gets tough, don't hesitate to reach out to the Alfreds in your life. Teachers, guidance counselors, and even your employers can be a great source of advice and support. Stuck on a tricky algebra problem? Ask your math teacher for help. Feeling overwhelmed by your work schedule? Talk to your boss or a coworker about it.

And then there's the power of peer support. Ever thought about joining or starting a study group? It's a great way to bounce ideas around and learn from each other. Also, consider finding a mentor or tutor - someone who's been in your shoes and can share their wisdom.

Balancing work and school isn't always a walk in the park, but with a little bit of self-care and the right support, you'll be cruising down that highway with the wind in your hair before you know it.

Fuel, Snooze, Move… And Repeat!

This might sound obvious, but let's be real, it's easy to overlook the basics when we're on the grind. So, a friendly nudge: ensure you're fueling up with healthy food (don't just survive on ramen or delivery pizza), getting some solid zzz's (aim for 7-9 hours, my friend), and moving your body. No, you don't have to be a gym rat. Simple stuff like a brisk walk, some chill yoga, or even shaking it off in your room (we won't judge, promise!) can do the trick!

Chill, Refresh, Power Up

Here's the lowdown on performing at your best: breaks aren't just nice-to-haves, they're must-haves. Your brain needs some chill time to process stuff and recharge, just like your phone needs a plug-in after a long day. So, make sure you're taking short breaks during your work or study sesh. Do something you love – jam out to your favorite tune, stroll around, or even daydream while cloud-watching for a bit. And hey, don't forget to take longer breaks too – weekends are meant for chilling, not just cramming in more work or study.

Reach Out: The Magic of Having Backup

Sure, you're strong and independent, but that doesn't mean you gotta do it all solo. Reach out to your pals, family, or mentors when things feel too much. Whether you need advice, a pep talk, or just an ear, don't hesitate to ask. Join a study group, sports team, hobby club, or just plan regular movie nights with friends — anything that keeps you plugged in and feeling supported.

Celebrate You

Last, but definitely not least, remember to give yourself a high-five now and then. Juggling work and school is a big deal, and you're totally rocking it. Celebrate your victories, no matter how small they seem. Nailed a tough work project? Crushed a test at school? Go ahead, do a little victory shimmy. You've totally earned it!

Remember, you can't fill from an empty jug. Looking after yourself isn't just good for your well-being; it's also key to killing it in both work and school. So, keep these pointers in your back pocket as you master this balancing act. You've totally got this!

Finding Your Balance: More Tips for Juggling School with Part-Time Jobs, Internships, Freelancing, and Entrepreneurship

Oh boy! You're not just a student—you're a student with a job, an intern, a freelancer, or even an entrepreneur. And that's quite a big deal! You're juggling school with real-life work and trying to excel at both. No worries, we've got you covered with some epic advice for each of these scenarios.

If you have a part-time job:

If you've scored a part-time job—kudos! It's not just about the extra cash (though it's a nice perk). You're learning real-world skills, and responsibility, and maybe getting a sneak peek into a potential career. To make this work:

Flex your negotiation skills: Talk to your boss about your work hours. Can they be tweaked around your study routine, especially when exams loom? Most bosses get it. After all, you're a student first.

Be wise with job selection: Go for jobs that sync with your study routine. Imagine working at a library or bookstore! You might get chances to hit the books during quiet hours. Not a bad deal, right?

If you're on an internship:

Internships offer a world of experience. You get to dip your toes into your field of study, and who knows, you might end up loving it! Here's how to make the best of internships:

Relevance is king: Choose internships that match your field of study. This way, you're not just learning at school but getting hands-on experience too. Imagine acing your exams because you actually did the stuff at your internship.

Timing is everything: Plan your internships during school breaks or when your academic load is lighter. This way, you won't miss out on either valuable experience or your school grades.

If you're freelancing on the side:

When you're a freelancer, you can choose what projects you take on, when you work, and where you work from. Here's how to balance this with school:

Time management is crucial: Set a work schedule and stick to it. Just because you can work anytime doesn't mean you should! Be clear with your clients about when you're available.

You're the boss: Pick projects that align with your skills, interests, and most importantly, your academic schedule. You're in charge here!

If you're starting a business while at school:

Starting your own venture while studying? That's incredibly brave and impressive! Here's how you can manage this tightrope act:

Delegate, delegate, delegate: You're the boss, but you don't have to do everything. Outsource tasks, hire people, use automation tools. Make your life easier!

Use your school: Your school isn't just for studying. It's a treasure trove of resources—mentors, networking events, entrepreneurship clubs. Use them to your advantage!

Remember, there's no one-size-fits-all strategy here. It's about trying different tactics, seeing what works for you, and not being afraid to make changes along the way. It might seem tricky at first, but you've totally got this. Just keep juggling and soon, you'll be a pro at the balancing act!

Chapter 14 - Parents, You've Got This! - Supporting Your Teen's Career Journey

"The greatest gift you can give your children are the roots of responsibility and the wings of independence." – Denis Waitley

Hey there, teens who have made it this far...

Before diving into this chapter, let's address the elephant in the room. You might be thinking, "Why is there a chapter for parents in a book that's supposed to be for me?" It's a fair question. While this book is primarily written for you, your parents play a crucial role in your life and your career journey. They have valuable experience, insights, and support to offer as you explore your interests, passions, and professional goals. So, let's work together to ensure that they're equipped to help you in the best way possible.

Alright, the following section is for your parents, but you're more than welcome to read it too. Knowledge is power, and understanding each other's perspectives can only strengthen your relationship.

Hello, Parents!

Thank you for taking the time to read this essential chapter. As your teen navigates the challenges and uncertainties of planning and pursuing their career, your guidance and support are more important than ever. As a parent, your primary goal is to help them grow into responsible, confident, and successful adults. While they might appear independent and mature at times, they still need you in ways they may not fully appreciate yet.

In today's fast-paced and competitive world, career exploration and decision-making can be overwhelming for both you and your teen. The landscape has changed significantly since you were in their shoes, and it's essential to adapt your approach accordingly. So, how can you best support your teen through this critical phase of their life and help them build a strong foundation for a successful career? The first step is to try and step into their shoes and understand their perspective and what they are going through.

Understanding, Supporting, and Guiding Your Teen's Journey

Understanding your teen's unique perspective is the cornerstone of effective support. As a parent, you've witnessed their growth and have insights into their strengths, weaknesses, and perhaps, their passions. However, it's crucial to remember that they are in a period of immense change and self-discovery. Their interests today may evolve tomorrow, and that's perfectly normal. The career journey is a winding path of self-discovery, not a straight line.

Your role in this phase isn't to dictate but to listen, understand, and guide gently. Encourage them to delve into their interests, even if these seem unconventional or unfamiliar to you. Their chosen career path should reflect their individuality, not societal expectations or stereotypes.

Crucial to this process is fostering a supportive environment at home.

Regular, open discussions about their aspirations, concerns, interests, and worries can go a long way. Show genuine curiosity about their day and dreams. Offer guidance without being overbearing and create a safe space where they feel heard and understood.

To further assist in their career exploration, provide them with the necessary resources. From online platforms, career counseling services, and mentorship programs to workshops and internships, there are numerous resources available today. Guide your teen towards these resources, but allow them to take the initiative to use them. Ownership of their career planning process is critical for their growth and confidence. You can find a comprehensive list of these in the resources chapter towards the end of the book. You never know, you might even discover something beneficial for yourself!

The world is evolving rapidly, and the skills required for success are changing just as quickly. Encourage your teen to develop a diverse skill set that includes both technical and soft skills. If they're interested in a particular field, help them find relevant courses, internships, or workshops. However, don't overlook the importance of soft skills like communication, teamwork, adaptability, and problem-solving. These skills are universally valuable and will serve them well in any career.

By understanding, supporting, and guiding your teen in this manner, you'll be well-equipped to help them navigate their unique career journey with confidence and optimism.

The job market your teenager is stepping into is totally different from the one you had to handle. It's super important you get these changes and use them to your advantage. Here's how you can tweak your game and help your teen ride this ever-changing wave:

Adapting to the New Career Scene

Your role as a parent or guardian in your teen's career quest is priceless. You're the rock and the cheering squad that pushes them to reach, learn, and explore. In this journey, it's crucial to realize that your teen's career scene might look pretty different from what you're used to - and that's totally cool.

This is the time of digital magic, artificial intelligence, and global connections, where new industries are popping up and old ones are shifting gears. The workforce is becoming super dynamic and diverse. Jobs are here today that we couldn't have dreamed of ten years ago, and likewise, careers will appear in the next decade that we can't even imagine right now.

So, how can you keep up with this shifting scene? Here are some tips:

1. Be in the Know: Put in the effort to understand the current job market by reading up, subscribing to newsletters that focus on career trends, and checking out webinars or forums on education and employment. Don't forget to share what you learn with your teen and chat about these trends.

2. Leverage Social Media: Social media can also be a crucial tool for staying updated on industry trends. Consider following thought leaders, companies, or groups within your teen's areas of interest. LinkedIn, for example, is a great spot for business and industry news.

3. Chat with Pros: Know someone who's in a field your teen is considering? Why not have a chat with them? Real-life insights can give a unique angle that articles and stats often miss.

4. Be Open to Fresh Opportunities: Remember, not all paths go straight from school to a stable, long-term job, and that's totally okay. Be open to different routes, like internships, freelancing, part-time gigs, or starting your own thing.

5. Use School Extras: Your teen's school is like a treasure chest of resources. Encourage them to chat with school career counselors, go to career fairs, and make use of any job placement services on offer.

By diving in to understand the changing career scene, you're loading up with the tools to better back your teen. Your guidance, combined with their grit and determination, will pave the way for a fulfilling career path that vibes with their interests and dreams.

Empowering Your Teen as They Forge Their Unique Career Path

Recognize and respect that your teen may choose a career path different from what you initially envisioned. Encourage them to independently explore different career options and industries, helping them take ownership of their career planning. Be open to new ideas and career possibilities, and support your teen in exploring these options. As your teen matures, they will strive for more independence, including in their career choices. Guide them, provide support, but also give them space to make their own decisions. Encourage your teen to consider all options, including non-traditional educational paths. Apprenticeships, trade schools, or even entrepreneurship could be the right fit for them.

Enhancing Communication and Understanding

Engage in open, honest, and constructive dialogues about their career aspirations and choices. Attend workshops, seminars, or parent-teacher conferences organized by your child's school, where you can learn more about the job market and the skills needed to succeed in different industries. Talk to other parents, colleagues, or friends about their experiences and insights into the job market. These conversations can provide you with a broader perspective, helping you better understand the challenges and opportunities your teen may face.

Navigating Financial Considerations for Your Teen's Future

As parents, it's totally normal to stress a bit about the cash side of your teen's education and career choices. The price tag on higher education and job training, as well as the potential payoff, can really weigh on your mind. Tackle these money matters head-on and team up with your teen to hatch a solid plan. Give your teen a hand researching different schools and job programs, comparing prices, and any financial aid that's up for grabs. Chat about the potential benefits of their chosen career path, including stuff like job openings, how much they could earn, and overall job satisfaction.

Snoop around for scholarships and grants that your teen might qualify for. Consider different education routes, like the community college route before switching to a four-year school or checking out online degree programs. These choices can be friendlier to your wallet and still lay a solid base for your teen's career. Give your teen a nudge to acquire valuable work experience through part-time jobs or internships that match their career interests. Finally, help your teen get savvy about money, teaching them the basics of budgeting, saving, and investing.

Building Resilience and Dealing with Setbacks

Let's face it, life is not always a picnic, and diving into the world of work is no exception. It's super important for your teen to understand that hiccups and hurdles are just part of the ride. In fact, it's often through these tough times that we grow the most! Here are some golden nuggets to help your teen become a master at handling life's curveballs and rebounding from setbacks stronger than ever:

Cheer on the Journey, Not Just the Destination: If your teen pours their heart into something, show them some love, no matter the result. This can help them see that it's about the journey, the learning, and the effort, not just the finish line.

Boost the 'Power of Yet': If your teen hasn't nailed a skill or hit a goal yet, remind them that they can, they just haven't yet. This 'power of yet' builds a growth mindset and helps them see potential roadblocks as temporary speed bumps, not dead ends.

Show Them that Failures are Stepping Stones: One of the best lessons you can share with your teen is to see failure as a stepping stone, not a pitfall. It's crucial to chat about how many big names have faced massive failures before they hit the jackpot.

Take J.K. Rowling, for example. She had to deal with loads of rejections and personal struggles before she became the author of one of the most successful book series ever – 'Harry Potter.' As a single mom battling poverty, Rowling's manuscript was turned down by twelve publishers before it finally got the thumbs up. If she had let her failures knock her down, we would never have discovered the magic of Hogwarts.

And let's not forget Walt Disney, whose first animation company went belly up, and he was even sacked from a newspaper gig for 'lacking ideas.' Crazy, right? This same guy went on to build a cartoon empire, gifting us unforgettable characters like Mickey Mouse and timeless classics like 'The Lion King.'

These stories prove that setbacks are not game over. In fact, they can often lead to bigger and better things. Sharing these tales can inspire your teen to view challenges and failures in a new light, sparking resilience and determination in their career journey.

Teach Them to Chill: Arm your teen with chill-out skills like mindfulness, deep breathing, or writing in a diary. These tools can help them handle stress and bounce back faster when life throws them a curveball. Speaking of, have you read our previous book The Essential Stress Management Handbook for Teens!

Promote Problem-Solving: When your teen hits a snag, guide them to brainstorm solutions rather than swooping in to save the day. This helps build resilience and faith in their problem-solving prowess.

Share Your Own Stories: Your own life tales can be a powerful lesson. Share times when you had to face the music and how you danced through it. This can help your teen see that everyone faces challenges and can beat them.

Most importantly, let your teen know that it's okay to feel bummed when things don't pan out. What matters is that they learn from these experiences and keep on truckin'. After all, being resilient isn't about never tripping up; it's about always standing back up.

We hope you've found "The Essential Career Planning Handbook for Teens" to be an invaluable resource in navigating the path to a successful future.

We're grateful for your time and dedication in reading our book, and we would be honored if you could spare a moment to share your thoughts with us.

Your feedback is not only valuable to us but also to other parents, educators, and teenagers who are seeking guidance in career planning. By leaving a review, you can help them make informed decisions and empower them to shape their own destinies.

We appreciate your support in spreading the word about the book and its impact. Remember, you have the power to inspire and motivate others on their journey to achieving their career aspirations. Together, let's equip the next generation with the tools and knowledge they need to succeed.

Thank you once again for being a valued reader, and we wish you nothing but the best in your career endeavors. Go forth and conquer your dreams with confidence!

Before We Say Goodbye!

W e hope you've found "The Essential Career Planning Handbook for Teens" to be an invaluable resource in navigating the path to a successful future. We're grateful for your time and dedication to reading our book, and we would be honored if you could spare just 60 seconds to share your thoughts with us.

Your feedback is not only valuable to us but also to other parents, educators, and teenagers who are seeking guidance in career planning. By leaving a review, you can help them make informed decisions and empower them to shape their own destinies.

We appreciate your support in spreading the word about the book and its impact. Remember, you have the power to inspire and motivate others on their journey to achieving their career aspirations. Together, let's equip the next generation with the tools and knowledge they need to succeed.

Customer reviews

⭐⭐⭐⭐⭐ 4.7 out of 5

221 global ratings

5 star	▓▓▓▓▓▓▓▓	76%
4 star	▓▓	20%
3 star	▏	3%
2 star		1%
1 star		1%

∨ How customer reviews and ratings work

Review this product

Share your thoughts with other customers

Write a customer review

Scan this QR code to leave a quick review!

Thank you once again for being a valued reader, and we wish you nothing but the best in your career endeavors. Go forth and conquer your dreams with confidence!

Conclusion

"Success is not final, failure is not fatal: It is the courage to continue that counts." – Winston Churchill

The Adventure is Just Beginning!

Well, look at you—you've zipped through this book! But let's make one thing crystal clear—this isn't the end of your epic journey. Nope, it's just the starting line. Your career, your future, and your big adventure are out there waiting, and trust me, it's going to be one for the books.

Remember the wise words of the legend Helen Keller who once said, "Life is either a daring adventure or nothing at all." You've got the power to make your life one heck of an adventure, loaded with hurdles to leap over, peaks to conquer, and wins to cheer about. Sure, you might trip and tumble along the way, but guess what? That's where the real lessons are. That's where you find your inner warrior.

You're not flying solo on this ride. You've got your crew—family, friends, mentors, and hey, even this book as your trusty sidekick. Don't be shy about asking for help, advice, or just an ear to vent when you need it. Your squad is there to boost you up and cheer you on every step of the journey.

Now, it's time to take everything you've absorbed from this book and bring it to life. Dive into your passions, build your skills, make connections, and open your eyes to the infinite opportunities that are waiting to be discovered. Don't just daydream about the future, start crafting it. Your journey is yours and yours alone—there's no 'one-size-fits-all' career path, so embrace the twists and turns and blaze your own trail.

And lastly, remember to relish the ride. This is your moment to explore, uncover, and evolve. It's your time to goof up, learn, and morph into the best version of yourself. Don't rush, don't stress, just keep cruising forward, one step at a time. You've totally got this!

So here's to you, brave explorer. Here's to your dreams, your future, and the extraordinary journey that's stretching out ahead. Now, let's get out there and shake things up. The world is waiting for you. Go show 'em what you're made of, champ!

Resources & Bibliography

Chapter 2 - Self Assessment and Introspection

Journaling Prompts for Self-Awareness

Here's a list of 20 prompts to help you with the self-awareness exercise. Feel free to think about each one or better yet type them out or jot them down in a notebook.

1. What are three qualities or strengths that you admire in yourself?

2. Reflect on a recent situation where you felt confident and in your element. What were the circumstances? How did it make you feel?

3. Describe a moment when you faced a challenge or obstacle. How did you handle it, and what did you learn from the experience?

4. What are three skills or talents that you believe set you apart from others?

5. Write about a time when you felt completely engaged and energized while doing a particular activity or pursuing a specific interest. What was it about that experience that made it so enjoyable?

6. List five values that are important to you in your personal and professional life. Explain why these values matter to you.

7. Reflect on a time when you achieved a significant goal or accomplishment. How did you feel when you achieved it? What steps did you take to reach that milestone?

8. Describe a situation where you felt a strong sense of purpose or meaning. What was it about that experience that made you feel connected to something greater than yourself?

9. Think about a career or profession that you find intriguing. What interests you about it? How do you imagine it aligning with your skills and passions?

10. Write about a time when you received feedback or recognition for your work. How did it make you feel, and what did you learn from the experience?

11. What are three areas where you feel you could improve or develop further? How do you plan to work on these areas?

12. Reflect on a moment when you took a risk or stepped outside of your comfort zone. What did you learn from that experience, and how did it contribute to your personal growth?

13. Describe an activity or hobby that brings you joy and allows you to express your creativity. How does engaging in this activity make you feel?

14. Write about a time when you made a mistake or faced failure. How did you handle it, and what did you learn from the experience?

15. What are three long-term goals you have for your career? How do these goals align with your values and aspirations?

16. Reflect on a mentor or role model who has had a significant impact on your life. What qualities or characteristics do you admire in them, and how have they inspired you?

17. Describe a situation where you had to collaborate with others to achieve a common goal. What role did you play in the team, and how did the experience contribute to your personal growth?

18. Write about a topic or subject that you enjoy learning about. How does gaining knowledge in this area make you feel, and how could it relate to potential career paths?

19. Reflect on a time when you felt a sense of accomplishment or fulfillment from helping others. How did it impact you, and how might you incorporate this aspect into your future endeavors?

20. Imagine yourself ten years from now. Describe your ideal career and life situation. What steps can you take now to move closer to that vision?

Use these prompts to explore and deepen your self-awareness through journaling.

Online Aptitude, Personality and Strengths Assessments

Here's an extensive list of aptitude, personality and strengths assessment tools and tests to help you in your career planning journey!

1. Myers-Briggs Type Indicator (MBTI): https://www.mbtionline.com/

2. StrengthsFinder: https://www.gallup.com/cliftonstrengths/en/home.aspx

3. Holland's Self-Directed Search (SDS): https://www.self-directed-search.com/

4. 16Personalities: https://www.16personalities.com/

5. CareerExplorer: https://www.careerexplorer.com/

6. VIA Character Strengths: https://www.viacharacter.org/

7. Big Five Personality Test: https://www.truity.com/test/big-five-personality-test

8. Keirsey Temperament Sorter: https://www.keirsey.com/

9. MindTools Career Test: https://www.mindtools.com/pages/career-test.htm

10. DISC Personality Test: https://www.123test.com/disc-personality-test/

11. Enneagram Test: https://www.truity.com/test/enneagram-personality-test

12. Values Assessment: https://www.mindtools.com/pages/article/newTED_85.htm

13. O*NET Interest Profiler: https://www.mynextmove.org/explore/ip

14. CareerOneStop Skills Matcher: https://www.careeronestop.org/toolkit/Skills/skills-matcher.aspx

15. PathSource: https://www.pathsource.com/

16. MyPlan.com: https://www.myplan.com/

17. CareerFitter: https://www.careerfitter.com/

18. Sokanu Career Test: https://www.sokanu.com/career-test/

19. JobQuiz: https://www.jobquiz.com/

20. LiveCareer Skills Assessment: https://www.livecareer.com/skills-assessment

These links offer a variety of online assessments and tools to help teenagers explore their aptitudes, personalities, and strengths. They can provide valuable insights and guidance for making informed career decisions.

Note: Some of the resources provided may require registration or payment for full access to the test results.

Chapter 3 - Charting Your Career Course: Navigating Towards Your Ideal Destination

Online Career Exploration and Job Search Resources

- My Next Move (www.mynextmove.org) - A comprehensive site for exploring careers based on your interests and skills.
- CareerOneStop (www.careeronestop.org) - Offers tools to explore careers, training, and job search resources.
- The Princeton Review (www.princetonreview.com/career-search) - Offers a career quiz and articles on various industries.
- Job Shadow (www.jobshadow.com) - Provides interviews with professionals in various fields to give you a glimpse into different careers.
- Inside Jobs (www.insidejobs.com) - Allows you to search for careers by

industry, field, or major.

- Glassdoor (www.glassdoor.com) - Offers insights into company culture, salaries, and job listings.
- LinkedIn (www.linkedin.com) - A professional networking site that can help you connect with professionals in your desired field and research companies.
- Monster (www.monster.com) - A popular job search website with articles and resources on various industries.
- Indeed (www.indeed.com) - A job search engine that can help you explore job listings and company reviews.
- Internships.com (www.internships.com) - A resource for finding internships in various industries.

Resources to Help You Learn About the Future of Work

- World Economic Forum (www.weforum.org) - Offers insights on the future of work, global trends, and emerging technologies.
- McKinsey Global Institute (www.mckinsey.com/mgi) - Conducts research on global economic issues, including the future of work and technological advancements.
- Wired (www.wired.com) - Covers the latest developments in technology and their potential impact on various industries and the job market.
- TechCrunch (www.techcrunch.com) - Focuses on emerging technology, startups, and their influence on the future job market.
- Singularity Hub (singularityhub.com) - Offers news and insights about emerging technologies and their potential impact on society and the job market.
- Future Today Institute (www.futuretodayinstitute.com) - A research-driven organization that provides insights on future trends, including work and technology.

- Forbes Future of Work (www.forbes.com/future-of-work) - A dedicated section on Forbes that covers the evolving job market, new technologies, and trends shaping the future of work.
- Fast Company (www.fastcompany.com) - A business media brand that covers innovation, technology, and the future of work.
- MIT Technology Review (www.technologyreview.com) - Offers insights on emerging technologies and their potential impact on the job market and society.
- Gartner (www.gartner.com) - A research and advisory company that provides insights on technology trends and their impact on businesses and the job market.

Podcasts:

1. WorkLife with Adam Grant (www.ted.com/podcasts/worklife) - Explores the minds of professionals and offers insights on work, leadership, and success.
2. The Ed Mylett Show (the-ed-mylett-show.simplecast.com) - Features interviews with successful people from various industries, discussing their career paths and insights on future trends.
3. The Future of Work Podcast with Jacob Morgan (thefutureorganizati on.com/future-work-podcast) - Covers topics related to the future of work, technology, and leadership.

These resources should provide a wealth of information to help teens learn about the evolving job market and stay informed about trends that could shape their future careers.

Online communities and forums

Here are a few resources you could suggest for this section:

1. **LinkedIn Groups**: There are numerous professional groups on LinkedIn that cater to various industries and career paths. These groups offer opportunities to network with professionals and gain insights into your chosen field.

2. **Reddit**: There are several subreddits dedicated to specific careers, industries, or topics like /r/careerguidance, /r/jobs, and /r/AskEngineers. They are great for asking questions, seeking advice, and hearing about others' experiences.

3. **Quora:** Similar to Reddit, Quora has a variety of topics where you can ask questions and get answers from industry professionals.

4. **Stack Exchange**: If you're interested in tech-related careers, Stack Exchange has several communities dedicated to specific topics in the tech industry.

5. **Meetup** (meetup.com): Although not strictly an online community, Meetup allows you to join groups with similar interests and often hosts events, which are currently mostly virtual due to the pandemic.

6. **Industry-specific forums**: For example, LawLink for legal professionals, Archinect for architects, and Behance for creative professionals.

7. **Discord Channels:** Many professional communities and industries have dedicated Discord channels for networking and discussion.

Remember to remind your readers that participating in online communities also means respecting the rules and guidelines of each platform, being polite, and maintaining professionalism even in informal online interactions.

Professional Associations, Industry Groups, and Online Communities

Certainly! Here is an extensive list of links and resources to supplement the section on professional associations, industry groups, and online communities:

Professional Associations:

1. American Marketing Association (AMA): https://www.ama.org/

2. National Society of Professional Engineers (NSPE): https://www.nspe.org/

3. Society for Human Resource Management (SHRM): https://www.shrm.org/

4. American Bar Association (ABA): https://www.americanbar.org/

5. American Institute of Architects (AIA): https://www.aia.org/

Industry Groups:

6. Women in Tech (WIT): https://www.womenintech.org/

7. Young Entrepreneurs Council (YEC): https://yec.co/

8. National Association of Black Journalists (NABJ): https://www.nabj.org/

9. Society of Women Engineers (SWE): https://swe.org/

10. National Association of Music Merchants (NAMM): https://www.namm.org/

Online Communities and Forums:

11. Reddit: Various subreddits dedicated to specific industries and professions, e.g., r/marketing, r/programming, r/finance

12. LinkedIn Groups: Join industry-specific LinkedIn Groups to connect with professionals and participate in discussions.

13. Stack Exchange: Q&A communities covering a wide range of topics, including programming (Stack Overflow), design (Stack Exchange - Graphic Design), and more.

14. Quora: A platform where professionals and experts answer questions related to various fields.

15. GitHub: Collaborative platform for developers to share and discuss code, projects, and ideas.

Additional Resources:

16. Meetup: Discover local events and groups related to your field of interest.

17. Eventbrite: Search for workshops, conferences, and networking events happening in your area or online.

18. TED Talks: Inspiring talks from experts in various fields, offering valuable insights and perspectives.

19. Coursera: Online courses from top universities and institutions to enhance your skills and knowledge.

20. Medium: A platform for professionals and thought leaders to share industry insights, career advice, and personal experiences.

These resources will help you connect with like-minded professionals, access valuable information, and stay updated on industry trends. Remember to actively participate, ask questions, and contribute to the discussions to make the most of these communities and groups. Happy networking and learning!

Chapter 4 - Understanding What It Takes to Achieve Your Dream

Career-Focused Websites

Here are some career-focused websites that you can refer to on your journey to your dream career:

1. LinkedIn (www.linkedin.com): LinkedIn is a professional networking platform that allows you to create a digital resume, connect with professionals in your field of interest, and discover job opportunities. It's a great place to build your professional network and learn from industry experts.

2. Indeed (www.indeed.com): Indeed is a popular job search engine where you can find job listings from various industries and locations. You can search for internships, entry-level positions, and even senior roles. It's a valuable resource to explore different career options and discover what qualifications employers are looking for.

3. Glassdoor (www.glassdoor.com): Glassdoor provides job listings, company reviews, and salary information. It offers insights into company cultures, interview experiences, and employee perspectives, helping you make more informed decisions about potential employers.

4. CareerOneStop (www.careeronestop.org): CareerOneStop, sponsored by the U.S. Department of Labor, provides a wide range of resources for career exploration and planning. It offers tools for assessing your skills and interests, exploring different occupations, and finding training and education programs.

5. The Muse (www.themuse.com): The Muse is a career advice and job search platform that offers articles, videos, and online courses to help you navigate your career journey. It provides insights into different industries, career paths, and job search strategies.

Remember to explore these websites and make the most of the resources they offer. They can provide valuable information, guidance, and inspiration as you work towards achieving your career aspirations.

Chapter 5 - Bridging the Gap: Leveling Up

Mastering the art of time management

Eisenhower Box: This is a productivity tool that helps you prioritize tasks based on their urgency and importance. It doesn't have an official website or app, but there are many variations available online and in app stores. Here's a good online version you can use: [Eisenhower Matrix](https://www.eisen hower.me/eisenhower-matrix/)

SMART Goals: This is a methodology for setting effective goals, and there's no specific tool or app for it. However, here's a good resource to understand how to set SMART goals: [SMART Goals - MindTools](https://www.mindto ols.com/pages/article/smart-goals.htm)

Google Calendar: This is a time-management and scheduling calendar service developed by Google. It can be accessed here: [Google Calendar](https://calendar.google.com/)

Todoist: This is a productivity app that helps manage tasks and projects. It can be accessed here: [Todoist](https://todoist.com/)

Trello: This is a collaboration tool that organizes your projects into boards, lists, and cards to keep your tasks organized and clear. It can be accessed here: [Trello](https://trello.com/)

Pomodoro Technique: This is a time management method that encourages taking regular breaks. There are numerous Pomodoro apps and online timers available. Here's a simple online one: [Pomodoro Tracker](https://pomodor o-tracker.com/)

Please note that the availability of these tools may vary by country, and some of them may require setting up a free account for access.

Exploring post high school education and training options

Vocational Schools:
1. Trade-Schools.net: https://www.trade-schools.net/
2. VocationalTrainingHQ: https://www.vocationaltraininghq.com/
3. Peterson's: https://www.petersons.com/vocational-careers

Community Colleges:
4. American Association of Community Colleges (AACC): https://www.aac c.nche.edu/
5. CommunityCollegeReview.com: https://www.communitycollegereview .com/

6. College Navigator - National Center for Education Statistics: https://nces.ed.gov/collegenavigator/

Apprenticeships:

7. Apprenticeship.gov: https://www.apprenticeship.gov/

8. Department of Labor Apprenticeship Finder: https://www.dol.gov/agencies/eta/apprenticeship/find-opportunities

Online Learning Platforms:

9. Coursera: https://www.coursera.org/

10. edX: https://www.edx.org/

11. Udacity: https://www.udacity.com/

Four-Year Colleges and Universities:

12. College Board: https://www.collegeboard.org/

13. Princeton Review: https://www.princetonreview.com/

14. U.S. News & World Report College Rankings: https://www.usnews.com/best-colleges

Financial Aid and Scholarships:

15. Federal Student Aid: https://studentaid.gov/

16. Fastweb: https://www.fastweb.com/

17. Scholarships.com: https://www.scholarships.com/

Additional Resources:

18. College Scorecard - U.S. Department of Education: https://collegescorecard.ed.gov/

19. Khan Academy: https://www.khanacademy.org/

20. BigFuture - The College Board: https://bigfuture.collegeboard.org/

These resources will provide valuable information about different education and training options, financial aid opportunities, and tools for researching and selecting the right path for your future. Remember to explore multiple resources, visit campuses, attend virtual events, and reach out to current students and professionals in your field of interest. Good luck on your educational journey!

Chapter 6 - Making the Career Plan!

Monitoring Your Progress

Certainly! Here is an extensive list of links and resources to supplement the section on monitoring your progress:

Productivity Apps and Tools:
1. Todoist: https://todoist.com/
2. Trello: https://trello.com/
3. Asana: https://asana.com/
4. Notion: https://www.notion.so/
5. Evernote: https://evernote.com/

Goal Tracking and Habit Building:
6. Habitica: https://habitica.com/
7. Strides: https://www.stridesapp.com/
8. Coach.me: https://www.coach.me/
9. Habitify: https://habitify.me/
10. StickK: https://www.stickk.com/

Progress Charts and Visual Tracking:
11. Canva: https://www.canva.com/
12. Google Sheets: https://www.google.com/sheets/about/
13. Microsoft Excel: https://www.microsoft.com/en-us/microsoft-365/excel

14. Airtable: https://airtable.com/

15. Notion: https://www.notion.so/

Self-Reflection and Journaling Apps:

16. Daylio: https://daylio.webflow.io/

17. Reflectly: https://reflectly.app/

18. Journey: https://journey.cloud/

19. Five Minute Journal: https://www.intelligentchange.com/products/five-minute-journal

20. Penzu: https://penzu.com/

These resources offer a variety of tools and apps to help you track your progress, set goals, and reflect on your journey. From productivity apps that help you stay organized and focused to habit trackers that assist you in building positive routines, these tools can enhance your self-monitoring efforts. Additionally, using visual aids like progress charts and utilizing journaling apps can provide a visual representation of your growth and enable self-reflection. Explore these resources and find the ones that best suit your preferences and needs.

Sample SMART Career Plan for an Aspiring Graphic Designer

CAREER PLAN FOR AN
ASPIRING GRAPHIC DESIGNER

01. Exploring Graphic Design

Specific: Research and learn about graphic design principles, tools, and career opportunities.

Measurable: Complete two online courses or workshops on graphic design fundamentals.

Achievable: Allocate 5 hours per week for self-study and learning.

Relevant: Gain a basic understanding of graphic design to make an informed career decision.

Time-bound: Complete the research and online courses within the next 3 months.

03. Build a Portfolio

Specific: Compile a portfolio of at least 10 design projects, including personal work and class assignments.

Measurable: Receive feedback from at least two design professionals or instructors.

Achievable: Dedicate time each week to work on portfolio projects.

Relevant: Showcase design skills and creativity to potential clients or employers.

Time-bound: Complete the portfolio and seek feedback within the next 6 months.

05. Refine Design Style and Approach

Specific: Experiment with different techniques and aesthetics to refine personal design style.

Measurable: Create and showcase three design projects exploring new styles or approaches.

Achievable: Dedicate time to creative exploration and learning from design resources.

Relevant: Continuously develop and improve design skills and creativity.

Time-bound: Complete the projects and self-reflection within the current academic year.

07. Freelancing and Building a Client Base

Specific: Offer freelance design services, network to attract clients, and deliver high-quality projects.

Measurable: Acquire at least five paying clients and complete design projects for each.

Achievable: Dedicate a set number of hours each week to freelance work and networking.

Relevant: Gain practical experience and build a reputation in the industry.

Time-bound: Acquire five clients and complete their projects within the next 12 months.

Age 14, Early High School

Age 14-16, Early High School

Age 15, Mid High School

Age 16, Late High School

Age 16-17, Late High School

Age 17, Late High School

Age 17-18, High School Graduation

Age 27+, Post High School & Career

02. Develop Design Skills

Specific: Enroll in two art and design courses, practice creating design projects, and improve technical skills.

Measurable: Complete a minimum of 5 design projects, showcasing different styles and techniques.

Achievable: Allocate 6 hours per week for coursework and practice.

Relevant: Build a strong foundation in design principles to enhance future career prospects.

Time-bound: Complete the courses and projects within the current academic year.

04. Gain Real Experience

Specific: Secure an internship or entry-level position at a design studio or agency.

Measurable: Complete at least three design projects under professional guidance.

Achievable: Submit applications to at least five relevant opportunities.

Relevant: Gain practical experience and develop industry connections.

Time-bound: Secure an internship or job offer within the next 9 months.

06. Establish a Personal Brand

Specific: Define a unique brand identity, create a professional website, and establish social media presence.

Measurable: Launch a website and establish social media profiles to showcase work and engage with the audience.

Achievable: Invest time and effort in branding and online presence development.

Relevant: Establish a professional image and attract potential clients or employers.

Time-bound: Launch the website and social media profiles within the next 3 months.

08. Set Up a Successful Graphic Design Agency

Specific: Establish a graphic design agency, hire a team of designers and administrative staff.

Measurable: Build a team with a minimum of five members to handle various aspects of the agency.

Achievable: Secure funding, develop a comprehensive business plan, and set up necessary infrastructure.

Relevant: Create a full-fledged graphic design agency to serve a diverse clientele.

Time-bound: Establish the agency within the next 3-5 years, with clear milestones for growth and expansion.

So, you might be wondering "What next after setting up the agency?". "Is that the end or just the beginning?"

No matter what stage you reach in your life, it's completely normal to want more. To want better. It's the human condition. The "final" destination is completely up to you.

A career destination you think is "final" today may only just be the beginning 10 or 15 years from now. So enjoy the process. Who knows what life has in store for you?

Chapter 8 - Nailing the Interviews

It's Showtime: Practice Makes Perfect

College interview questions:

In general, U.S. college admissions interviews typically consist of a single round. However, the process may vary depending on the specific institution and the type of program to which a student is applying. Some colleges may not require interviews at all, while others may conduct interviews on an invitation-only basis, often for more competitive programs or scholarships.

It's essential to research the specific college and program you're applying to and understand their interview process. If an interview is required or recommended, it's usually a one-on-one conversation with an admissions officer, alumni interviewer, or current student. The purpose of the interview is to learn more about the applicant, assess their interpersonal skills, and gauge their interest in the school.

1. Tell me about yourself.
2. Why are you interested in this part-time job?
3. What skills or experiences do you have that make you a good fit for this position?
4. Can you discuss a challenging situation you've faced at work or school and how you overcame it?
5. What are your strengths and weaknesses?
6. What days and hours are you available to work? Are you available on weekends or holidays?
7. Can you give an example of when you've demonstrated teamwork or collaboration?
8. How do you handle difficult customers or resolve conflicts?
9. How do you stay organized and manage your time effectively?
10. Are you familiar with our company/organization? What do you know about us?
11. How do you plan to contribute to our company/organization during your time here?
12. Can you discuss a project, assignment, or work task you've completed that you're particularly proud of?
13. How would your friends, classmates, or coworkers describe you?
14. Do you have experience using any specific tools, software, or equipment relevant to this position?
15. Do you have any questions for me about the part-time job or our company/organization?

Internship/Part time job interview questions

1. Tell me about yourself.
2. Why are you interested in this part-time job?
3. What skills or experiences do you have that make you a good fit for this position?

4. Can you discuss a challenging situation you've faced at work or school and how you overcame it?
5. What are your strengths and weaknesses?
6. What days and hours are you available to work? Are you available on weekends or holidays?
7. Can you give an example of when you've demonstrated teamwork or collaboration?
8. How do you handle difficult customers or resolve conflicts?
9. How do you stay organized and manage your time effectively?
10. Are you familiar with our company/organization? What do you know about us?
11. How do you plan to contribute to our company/organization during your time here?
12. Can you discuss a project, assignment, or work task you've completed that you're particularly proud of?
13. How would your friends, classmates, or coworkers describe you?
14. Do you have experience using any specific tools, software, or equipment relevant to this position?
15. Do you have any questions for me about the part-time job or our company/organization?

Here's a list of common internship interview questions that teens should practice:

1. Tell me about yourself.
2. Why are you interested in this internship?
3. What skills or experiences do you have that make you a good fit for this internship?
4. Can you discuss a challenging situation you've faced and how you overcame it?
5. What are your strengths and weaknesses?
6. How do your academic and extracurricular activities relate to this

internship?

7. Can you give an example of when you've demonstrated leadership or teamwork?

8. What are your long-term career goals or aspirations?

9. How do you handle stress or manage your time effectively?

10. What do you hope to gain from this internship experience?

11. How would your friends, classmates, or professors describe you?

12. Are you familiar with our company/organization? What do you know about us?

13. How do you plan to contribute to our company/organization during your internship?

14. Can you discuss a project or assignment you've completed that you're particularly proud of?

15. Do you have any questions for me about the internship or our company/organization?

Practicing your responses to these questions will help you confidently and effectively communicate your experiences, goals, and qualifications during an internship interview.

Chapter 9 - Making Connections: Networking

Finding Careers Fairs Near You

Certainly! Here's an extensive list of links and resources to supplement the section on mastering career fair networking:

1. Eventbrite: A platform that lists various career fairs and networking events happening in different locations. (https://www.eventbrite.com/)

2. Handshake: A career platform that connects students with employers and lists career fairs and networking events. (https://www.joinhandshake.com/)

3. National Career Fairs: Offers information on upcoming career fairs held in major cities across the United States. (https://www.nationalcareerfairs.com/)

4. The Balance Careers: Provides a guide on finding and attending career fairs, including tips for success. (https://www.thebalancecareers.com/how-to-find-and-attend-career-fairs-2059576)

5. My Next Move: Offers a career fair finder tool to search for upcoming events by location and industry. (https://www.mynextmove.org/)

6. National Association of Colleges and Employers (NACE): Provides resources and information on career fairs and networking opportunities for college students and graduates. (https://www.naceweb.org/)

7. Professional Association Websites: Visit the websites of professional associations in your field of interest to discover career fairs and networking events they organize. Examples include the American Marketing Association, Society for Human Resource Management, or National Society of Professional Engineers.

8. College and University Career Centers: Check out the career center websites of colleges and universities in your area to find information on upcoming career fairs and networking events specific to students and alumni.

Remember to regularly check these resources and websites for updated information on career fairs and networking events. Additionally, your school or college career center can be a valuable source of information and guidance for finding relevant opportunities.

Chapter 11 - The Amazing World of Freelancing

Online Freelance Marketplaces

Here are some online freelance marketplaces where you can find freelance opportunities:

1. Upwork (https://www.upwork.com/): A platform for freelancers of all types, from writers and designers to accountants and marketers.

2. Fiverr (https://www.fiverr.com/): A marketplace where freelancers can offer their services in packages called "gigs".

3. Freelancer (https://www.freelancer.com/): This platform hosts millions of projects in areas like website development, writing, design, and more.

4. Guru (https://www.guru.com/): Another comprehensive freelance marketplace with a wide range of categories.

5. Toptal (https://www.toptal.com/): A freelance platform that connects top freelancers with innovative startup companies.

6. Behance (https://www.behance.net/): Ideal for creative professionals, such as graphic designers and illustrators.

7. Dribbble (https://dribbble.com/): A platform for designers showcasing their work and finding freelance opportunities.

8. 99Designs (https://99designs.com/): A freelance marketplace for graphic design work.

9. PeoplePerHour (https://www.peopleperhour.com/): This platform connects freelancers with businesses who need their skills.

10. ProBlogger Job Board (https://problogger.com/jobs/): An excellent resource for freelance writing and blogging gigs.

11. SimplyHired (https://www.simplyhired.com/): A job search engine that also includes freelance and remote work opportunities.

12. FlexJobs (https://www.flexjobs.com/): A job search site specializing in remote, part-time, freelance, and flexible jobs.

Remember, it's important to read the terms and conditions of each platform before you sign up, as they may have different fee structures and policies.

Resources and Support for Teen Freelancers

So, you're all set to rock the freelance world, eh? Awesome! Guess what? There's a whole universe of resources and support waiting just for you. These nifty tools can help you polish your skills, score cool gigs, and connect with others who are as jazzed about freelancing as you are. Let's check 'em out!

Books and blogs: Remember, knowledge is your secret weapon! There's a mountain of excellent books and blogs out there that can teach you the A to Z of freelancing—from marketing your services to managing your moolah. Some must-reads include "The Freelancer's Bible" by Sara Horowitz and "My So-Called Freelance Life" by Michelle Goodman. Don't forget to surf the web for insightful blog posts and articles too!

Online classes and workshops: Ready to upgrade your skills? Online courses and workshops are the way to go. Websites like Udemy, Coursera, and

Skillshare offer a buffet of courses in everything from coding to creative writing. And guess what? They often have sweet deals for students, so you could bag a discount!

Social media circles and forums: Chatting with other freelancers is a superb way to get tips, share your journey, and learn from folks who've walked in your shoes. Check out Facebook groups, Reddit threads, and other online forums meant for freelancers. Just remember to respect the rules of the group and treat everyone nicely—we're all on the same team here!

Freelance job sites: Hunting for gigs can be a challenge, but freelance job platforms can make it a breeze. Websites like Upwork, Freelancer, and Fiverr are popular hotspots where you can create a snazzy profile, flaunt your portfolio, and bid on jobs. Just remember, it's a competitive world out there, so make sure your profile is a real head-turner!

Meet-ups and networking events: Getting to know other freelancers and industry pros in real life is a fantastic way to build your network and learn from others. Keep your eyes peeled for local networking events, workshops, or meetups in your neighborhood. Websites like Meetup.com or Eventbrite can help you find events that vibe with your interests.

Mentorship: Sometimes, having a mentor who's been there, done that, can be a game-changer. Don't hesitate to reach out to people in your network or in the freelance world who you look up to. Ask if they'd be cool with offering guidance or advice. You might be surprised at how many people are ready to help a young freelancer just getting started!

Chapter 12 - Considering Entrepreneurship: An Introduction to Starting Your Own Venture

Helpful Stuff for Young Business Whizzes: Books, Websites, and More

Hey there, future business superstar! So, you're all set to embark on your entrepreneurship adventure. But guess what? You don't have to go at it alone! There are plenty of resources out there just waiting to help you shine. Let's check out a few of them.

Books: Your Brain Food

Books are like the ultimate brain fuel for entrepreneurs like you. They're jam-packed with knowledge and cool stuff that can help you grow and succeed. Check out "The Lean Startup" by Eric Ries, a fantastic read about building a successful business. If you're into the tech world, dive into "Zero to One" by Peter Thiel for an inside look at startups. And don't forget "Rich Dad Poor Dad" by Robert Kiyosaki, a book all about financial wisdom.

Websites: The World at Your Fingertips

The internet is like a treasure trove of information, and there are websites that are perfect for young entrepreneurs like you. Check out Entrepreneur.com and YoungEntrepreneur.com for useful articles and tips to kick-start your journey. And for free online courses on entrepreneurship and business, platforms like Coursera and Khan Academy have got you covered.

Organizations: Your Potential Business Buddies

Sometimes, having a team by your side can make all the difference. That's where organizations like the Young Entrepreneur Council and the Future

Business Leaders of America come in. They're specifically designed for young entrepreneurs like you, offering advice, mentorship, and amazing networking opportunities.

Remember, these resources are like your guides, mentors, and biggest cheerleaders as you venture into the exciting world of entrepreneurship. So, dive right in, soak up all the knowledge you can, and get ready to rock your entrepreneurial dreams. Your future self will thank you for taking the leap!

Chapter 13 - Parents, You've Got This! - Supporting Your Teen's Career Journey

Here are several resources that could be helpful to parents supporting their teen's career journey:

1. American School Counselor Association (ASCA) (https://www.schoolcoun selor.org/): Offers a variety of resources for parents about the role of school counselors and how they can assist in career planning.

2. CareerOneStop (https://www.careeronestop.org/): Sponsored by the U.S. Department of Labor, this site provides a wealth of career, training, and job search resources for parents and teens.

3. Bureau of Labor Statistics (BLS) Occupational Outlook Handbook (https://w ww.bls.gov/ooh/): Offers detailed information about various careers, including education requirements, job outlook, typical duties, and more.

4. The College Board (https://www.collegeboard.org/): Provides resources for college planning, including information on SAT/ACT testing, college search tools, and scholarship opportunities.

5. Federal Student Aid (https://studentaid.gov/): An office of the U.S. Department of Education providing information on preparing for college, types of aid available, how to apply for aid, and how to manage loans.

6. National Association for College Admission Counseling (NACAC) (https://www.nacacnet.org/): Offers advice for parents on college admission, financial aid, and more.

7. Career Key (https://www.careerkey.org/): A career decision-making tool that can help teens explore different career options based on their interests and personality.

8. Common Sense Media (https://www.commonsensemedia.org/): Provides advice on safe and appropriate media for kids and teens, including educational online resources.

9. Khan Academy (https://www.khanacademy.org/): Offers free online courses in various subjects, which can be useful for skill building and exploration.

10. Coursera (https://www.coursera.org/): An online platform offering courses from top universities and companies that can help teens explore different fields.

11. edX (https://www.edx.org/): Provides free online courses from leading institutions worldwide.

12. LinkedIn Learning (https://www.linkedin.com/learning/): Offers courses in a wide range of professional skills, which could be useful for older teens considering certain career paths.

13. Parent Toolkit (https://www.parenttoolkit.com/): Provides advice on academic growth and personal development for kids from pre-K through

high school.

Remember, it's also important to connect with your local community resources like school counselors, career centers, local colleges, and libraries, which often have resources for college and career planning.

About the Author

Richard Meadows is the founder of RaiseYouthRight, a publishing company dedicated to sharing practical wisdom that empowers the next generation to lead healthier, wealthier, and happier lives. As a bestselling author and mentor to teens, Richard combines his personal experience as a teenager with his passion for guiding young people.

His books, including the highly acclaimed "The Essential Social Skills Handbook for Teens," tackle crucial topics such as social anxiety, confidence building, stress management, and academic and mindset guidance. Richard's unique approach is tailored to the specific needs of teenagers and young adults, providing clear and relatable guidance they can implement in their daily lives.

Having experienced his own struggles with self-esteem, confidence, and social anxiety during his youth, Richard understands firsthand the challenges faced by teenagers today. He embarked on a personal journey of self-discovery, utilizing the strategies he learned through reading and applying them to heal and grow.

Recognizing that not all young people have access to the support they need,

Richard is driven to make a difference through his writing. His ultimate goal is to ensure that practical guidance and resources are readily available to every teenager seeking to overcome their obstacles and thrive in their journey toward adulthood. With RaiseYouthRight, Richard is on a mission to inspire and empower the next generation to reach their full potential.

You can connect with me on:

- https://raiseyouthright.com
- https://twitter.com/raiseyouthright
- https://www.facebook.com/raiseyouthright

Also by RaiseYouthRight

Richard Meadows is the founder of RaiseYouthRight, a publishing company dedicated to sharing practical wisdom that empowers the next generation to lead healthier, wealthier, and happier lives. As a bestselling author and mentor to teens, Richard combines his personal experience as a teenager with his passion for guiding young people.

His books, including the highly acclaimed "The Essential Social Skills Handbook for Teens," tackle crucial topics such as social anxiety, confidence building, stress management, and academic and mindset guidance. Richard's unique approach is tailored to the specific needs of teenagers and young adults, providing clear and relatable guidance they can implement in their daily lives.

Having experienced his own struggles with self-esteem, confidence, and social anxiety during his youth, Richard understands firsthand the challenges faced by teenagers today. He embarked on a personal journey of self-discovery, utilizing the strategies he learned through reading and applying them to heal and grow.

Recognizing that not all young people have access to the support they need, Richard is driven to make a difference through his writing. His ultimate goal is to ensure that practical guidance and resources are readily available to every teenager seeking to overcome their obstacles and thrive in their journey toward adulthood. With RaiseYouthRight, Richard is on a mission to inspire and empower the next generation to reach their full potential.

The Essential Stress Management Handbook for Teens

Discover the ultimate stress management guide designed specifically for teens in the post-pandemic era. In "The Essential Stress Management Handbook for Teens," you'll unlock the keys to conquering stress and empowering your teens to thrive. With practical strategies, proven techniques, and personalized advice, this book equips both teens and parents with the tools they need to navigate the pressures of school, digital overload, and social challenges. From agile stress-relief techniques to habit-forming exercises, you'll learn how to transform stress-busting hacks into natural instincts that empower your teens to tackle stress head-on. Don't let stress hinder your teens' happiness and success—grab your copy today and embark on a journey toward a stress-free and fulfilling life.

The Essential Social Skills Handbook for Teens

Unlock your teen's full potential with "The Essential Social Skills Handbook for Teens." If your teen struggles with anxiety, lack of confidence, or shyness, this book is the transformative solution you've been searching for. Written by an author who has personally overcome these challenges, this handbook offers practical techniques and valuable insights to boost your teen's confidence in just 30 days. Say goodbye to social anxieties and hello to a new level of self-assurance. From effective communication strategies to mastering social interactions, this book covers it all. With proven methods and bonus templates, your teen will develop the skills needed to thrive in social situations, set goals, and unleash their true potential. Don't let your teen miss out on the opportunity to become the socially confident individual they deserve to be.

Made in United States
Troutdale, OR
12/03/2024

25482685R00139